George Valentine Yool

An Essay on Waste, Nuisance and Trespass

Chiefly with Reference to Remedies in Equity

George Valentine Yool

An Essay on Waste, Nuisance and Trespass
Chiefly with Reference to Remedies in Equity

ISBN/EAN: 9783337813079

Printed in Europe, USA, Canada, Australia, Japan

Cover: Foto ©Suzi / pixelio.de

More available books at **www.hansebooks.com**

AN ESSAY

ON

WASTE, NUISANCE, AND TRESPASS,

CHIEFLY WITH REFERENCE TO REMEDIES IN EQUITY;

TREATING OF THE LAW OF

TIMBER, MINES, LIGHTS, WATER, SUPPORT, THE CONSTRUCTION OF PUBLIC WORKS, &c., &c.

BY

GEORGE V. YOOL, M.A.,

OF LINCOLN'S INN, BARRISTER-AT-LAW, LATE FELLOW OF TRINITY COLLEGE, CAMBRIDGE.

LONDON:

W. MAXWELL, 32, BELL YARD, LINCOLN'S INN,

Law Bookseller and Publisher.

HODGES, SMITH, & CO., DUBLIN; BELL & BRADFUTE, EDINBURGH.

1863.

CONTENTS.

CHAPTER I.

WASTE.

CHAPTER II.

NUISANCE.

CHAPTER III.

TRESPASS.

CHAPTER IV.

CONSTRUCTION OF PUBLIC WORKS.

TABLE OF CASES.

C.

D.

H.

I.

L.

M.

Q.

R.

T.

U.

V.

W.

Y.

ADDENDA ET CORRIGENDA.

Page	27 n. 4.	Add, *Blewett* v. *Jenkins*, 12 C. B. N. S. 16.
,,	48 n. 5.	*Blake* v. *Peters*, V.-C. K., reported 10 W. R. 826.
,,	53 n. 9.	*Lord Lovat* v. *Duchess of Leeds*, reported 2 Dr. & S. 75.
,,	55 n. 3.	Add, *Spencer* v. *Scurr*, M. R. 10 W. R. 878, 31 L. J. Ch. 808.
,,	58 n. 5.	*Blake* v. *Peters*, V.-C. K., reported 10 W. R. 826.
,,	60 n. 3.	Do. do.
	86 n. 7.	Add, *Attorney-General* v. *Conservators of the Thames*, 1. N. R. 121; *Kearns* v. *Cordwainer's Company*, 6 C. B. N. S. 388.
,,	86 n. 9.	*Attorney-General* v. *Electric Telegraph Company*, reported 30 Beav. 287.
,,	88 n. 7.	See, now, 25 & 26 Vict. c. 42.
,,	96 n. 4.	Add, *Bidder* v. *Croydon Board of Health*, 6 L. T. N. S, 778.
,,	96 n. 9.	Add, *Attorney-General* v. *Conservators of the Thames*, V.-C. W., 1 N. R. 121
,,	101 n. 4.	Add, *Daniel* v. *Anderson*, 31 L. J. Ch. 610. *Dodd* v. *Burchall*, 31 L. J. Ex. 364.
,,	102 n. 7.	*White* v. *Bass*, reported 7 H. & N. 722.
,,	108 n. 2.	Add, *Cooper* v. *Hubbuck*, 6 L. T. N. S. 826.
,,	112 n. 8.	Add, *Jones* v. *Tapling*, in error, 31 L. J. C. P. 342.
,,	121 n. 6.	*Beardmore* v. *Tredwell*, reported 31 L. J. Ch. 892.
,,	138 n. 5.	Add, *Bidder* v. *Croydon Board of Health*, 6 L. T. N. S. 778.
,,	158 n. 2.	Add, *North Eastern Railway Company* v. *Crosland*, 1 N. R. 72.
,,	164 n. 6.	*Bennett* v. *Great Western Railway Company*, 1 N. R. 164.
,,	170 n. 7.	*Blackett* v. *Broadley*, reported 1 B. & S. 940.
,,	172 n. 5.	*Newton* v. *Cubitt*, reported 12 C. B. N. S. 32.

Page 172 n. 6. *Attorney-General* v. *Electric Telegraph Company*, reported 30 Beav. 287.

,, 179 n. 9. Do. do.

,, 191 n. 6. *Perks* v. *Wycombe Railway Company*, on appeal, 1 N. R. 1.

,, 196 n. 2. *Attorney-General* v. *Electric Telegraph Company*, reported 30 Beav. 287.

,, 216 nn. 2 & 3. Add, *Bedford and Cambridge Railway Company* v. *Stanley*, V.-C. W., 5th December, 1862.

,, 220 n. 6. Add, *Lind* v. *Isle of Wight Ferry Company*, 1 N. R. 13. *Mason* v. *Stokes Bay Railway Company*, 1 N. R. 84.

,, 222 n. 6. *Perks* v. *Wycombe Railway Company*, on appeal, 1 N. R. 1.

,, 223 n. 5. Add, *Caledonian Railway Company* v. *Lockhart*, 3 Macq. 808.

,, 224 n. 2. Add, *Bagnall* v. *London and North Western Railway Company*, 7 H. & N. 423, in Ex. C. 10 W. R. 802, 31 L. J. Ex. 480.

,, 225 n. 7. *Chamberlaine* v. *West End and Crystal Palace Railway Company*, on appeal pending.

,, 226 line 14. As to whether the landowner's remedy is by injunction, damages, or compensation, see *Wedmore* v. *Corporation of Bristol*, 1 N. R. 120.

,, 234 line 8. It seems that where no part of the lands of a tenant from year to year are taken, but his interest in the lands is injuriously affected by the works, compensation is to be assessed under the 68th section, before a jury or arbitrators, and not by justices. *Somers* v. *Metropolitan Railway Company*, 31 L. J. Q. B. 261.

,, 245 line 9. See *Attorney-General* v. *Conservators of the Thames*, 1 N. R. 121.

A

TREATISE

ON

WASTE, NUISANCE, AND TRESPASS.

CHAPTER I.

Chap. I.

WASTE.

1. *Legal Waste.*
2. *Equitable Waste.*
3. *General matters relating to Waste.*
4. *Waste in timber and other trees and underwood.*
5. *Waste in minerals, &c.*
6. *Waste in buildings.*
7. *Landlord and Tenant.*
8. *Mortgagor and Mortgagee.*
9. *Ecclesiastical Corporations.*

Sect. 1.—LEGAL WASTE.

Sect. 1.

Waste, what it is.

The principle upon which waste depends is thus stated in the case of *Lord Darcy* v. *Askwith.*[1] "It is generally true that the lessee hath no power *to change the nature of the thing demised;*

[1] Hob. 234.

CHAP. I.
Sect. 1.

he cannot turn meadow into arable,[2] nor stub a wood to make it pasture, nor dry up an ancient pool or piscary, nor suffer ground to be surrounded, nor decay the pale of park, for then it ceaseth to be a park, nor he may not destroy or drive away the stock or breed of anything, because it disherits and takes away the perpetuity of succession, as villains, fish, deer,[3] young spring of woods, or the like, but he may better a thing of the same kind, as by digging a meadow to make a drain or sewer to carry away water."

Substantial damage.

It appears, however, that the consequences of waste do not attach, unless substantial damage is done to the inheritance, which may be either, (1) By diminishing the value of the estate; (2) By increasing the burthen upon it; (3) By impairing the evidence of title.[4]

Meliorating waste.

An act which increases the value of the estate

[2] Toth. 114, 209, 210; *Atkyns* v. *Temple*, Chan. Rep. 13; *Basset* v. *Basset*, Fin. Rep. 189; *Worsley* v. *Stuart*, 4 Bro. P. C., 2nd edit. p. 377; *Duke of St. Albans* v. *Skipwith*, 8 Beav. 354.

[3] As to reclaiming deer, see *Morgan* v. *Abergavenny*, 8 C. B. 768; *Ford* v. *Tynte*, 2 J. & H. 150; and for battery of villains, 22 Vin. Abr. 488

[4] *Doe* v. *Earl of Burlington*, 5 B. & Adol. 507; *Harrow School* v. *Alderton*, 2 B. & P. 86; *Huntley* v. *Russell*, 13 Jur. 837; 18 L. J. Q. B. 239; 13 Q. B. 572.

may be waste, if it damages the inheritance in either the second or third of the above modes. Such acts are termed Meliorating waste.[5]

Waste may be voluntary or permissive.

Waste is either voluntary or permissive. Voluntary waste consists in the commission of acts which the tenant has no authority to do, such as pulling down buildings, felling timber, or opening mines. Permissive waste arises from the omission of acts which it is the tenant's duty to do, as, for example, suffering buildings to go to decay, by wrongfully neglecting to repair them.[6]

Action of waste.

An action of waste is said by Lord Coke to lie against tenant by the curtesie, tenant in dower, tenant for life, or years, or half-a-year, or guardian in chivalry by him that hath the immediate estate of inheritance for waste done to his disherison.[7]

Against whom action lay at common law.

The remedy against waste by guardian in chivalry, tenant in dower, and tenant by the

[5] 2 Will. Saunders, 259; *Simmons* v. *Norton*, 7 Bing. 640; *Wild* v. *Straddling*, Finch, 135; *Ligo* v. *Smith*, 2 Vern. 263; *Molineux* v. *Powell*, 3 P. W. 268, *n.*; *Barry* v. *Barry*, 1 J. & W. 651; *Duke of Leeds* v. *Earl Amherst*, 2 Ph. 117; *Morris* v. *Morris*, 3 D. & J. 323; *Coppinger* v. *Gubbins*, 3 J. & L. 397; 9 Ir. Eq. 304; *Doran* v. *Carroll*, 11 Ir. Ch. 397.

[6] Co. Litt. 53 a; 1 Inst. 145; *White* v. *M'Cann*, 1 Ir. C. L. 205.

[7] Co. Litt. 53 a.

curtesie, was given by the common law because their estates were created by the law itself. But until the statutes of Marlbridge[8] and Gloucester,[9] there was no protection against tenants for life or years, because they came in by act of the parties, and the settlor might have provided against the commission of waste by them.[1]

Who may bring the action.

It will have been remarked that the action can only be brought by one who has the immediate estate of inheritance, *i. e.*, an immediate reversion or remainder in fee or in tail. Thus, "If a lease be made to A. for life or years, remainder to B. for life, and A. commit waste, the action cannot be brought by him in the remainder, or reversion in fee or in tail, so long as the estate of B. continues.[2] But if B. should afterwards die or surrender his estate, the reversioner or remainderman may bring an action against A. for the waste so done by him, for by the death or surrender of B. the impediment is removed.[3] So

[8] 52 H. 3, c. 23.

[9] 6 Edw. 1, c. 5.

[1] 2 Inst. 301.

[2] Co. Litt. 54 a; *Udal* v. *Udal*, Aleyn, 81; 2 Rol. Abr. 829; *Bray* v. *Tracy*, Cro. Jac. 688; W. Jones, 51.

[3] Moore, 387; *Paget's Case*, 5 Rep. 76 b; *Bray* v. *Tracy*, Cro. Jac. 688; W. Jones, 51.

if a lease for life be made, remainder for years, the reversioner or remainderman may bring the action notwithstanding the mesne remainder.[4] No person can maintain the action unless he had an estate of inheritance in him at the time of the waste committed, and therefore it does not lie by an heir for waste done in the lifetime of his ancestor,[5] nor by the grantee of a reversion for waste done before the grant to him."[6] But for waste done before a recovery the quondam tenant in tail might have brought waste after the recovery.[7]

Action on the case.

The foregoing observations are to be understood in the first instance of the action of waste,[8] but they appear to be also applicable to the action on the case which has been substituted for it.[9]

Waste by a stranger.

It is presumed in law that the tenant can pre-

[4] Co. Litt. 54 a; 2 Inst. 301; 2 Rol. Abr. 829.

[5] 2 Inst. 305 a; *Bacon* v. *Smith*, 1 Q. B. 345; 6 P. & D. 651.

[6] 2 Will. Saunders, 252; Notes to *Greene* v. *Cole*.

[7] *Garth* v. *Cotton*, 3 Atk. 751; 1 Ves. S. 524, 546; 1 Dick. 183; 1 W. & T. Lead. Ca.; *Doe* v. *Scarborough*, 3 A. & E. 15, 923.

[8] Abolished 3 & 4 Will. 4, c. 27, s. 26; the most recent examples of this action are *Harrow School* v. *Alderton*, 2 B. & P. 86; *Redfern* v. *Smith*, 1 Bing. 382.

[9] *Jefferson* v. *Jefferson*, 3 Lev. 131; *Bacon* v. *Smith*, 1 Q. B. 345; 4 P. & D. 651.

CHAP. I. Sect. 1.

vent a stranger from committing waste. In such a case, therefore, the reversioner has an action of waste against the tenant and the tenant has trespass over against the wrong-doer.[1] Moreover, when the waste consists in cutting down and carrying away a tree or the like, the reversioner may have trover for it, the special property of the tenant in the tree ceasing upon severance.[2] The reversioner has also an action against the stranger for the injury done to the reversion.[3]

Tenant in tail after possibility.

A tenant in tail after possibility of issue extinct, cannot bring an action for waste as a remainderman of inheritance, because he is in effect but tenant for life, but he may commit waste when he comes himself into possession.[4]

Husband of lessee.

The husband of a lessee for life is solely responsible for acts of waste committed during the coverture.[5]

Copyholds

It is said that an action for waste will lie by a

[1] 2 Inst. 146; see *Lady Evelyn's Case*, 2 Freem. 55; 2 Swanst. 172.

[2] *Berry* v. *Heard*, Cro. Car. 242; *Anon.*, 1 Ves. J. 93; see post, Sect. 4.

[3] 3 Lev. 130; 3 Lev. 209; 1 Taunt. 183; see as to injunction, post, "Trespass," Sect. 1.

[4] 2 Rol. Abr. 825, 826; Co. Litt. 28 a, 53 b; 2 Inst. 301, and post, p. 9.

[5] *Kingham* v. *Lee*, 15 Sim. 396.

copyholder in remainder against a copyholder for life, but not by the lord of a manor against his copyhold tenants.[6]

Leases renewable for ever.

It has been settled (in Ireland), after considerable doubt, that the holder of a lease for lives, renewable for ever, is not at liberty to commit destructive waste: but it seems that he may commit meliorating waste.[7]

Without impeachment of waste.

There is incident to every estate for life or for years, the right to take estovers, that is to say, so much wood, stone, &c., as is required for use on the tenement for repairs, husbandry, and such like purposes. But it is a common practice in family settlements to provide that in addition to this privilege the estates of the tenants for lives shall be "without impeachment of waste." The effect of this clause is both to discharge any action for waste,[8] and also to give the tenant the property in timber, minerals, &c., severed by

[6] Scriven, 4th edit. p. 424—444. The latter part of the proposition is probably erroneous, *Parrott* v. *Palmer*, 3 M. & K. 639.

[7] *Coppinger* v. *Gubbins*, 3 J. & L. 397; 9 Ir. Eq. R. 304; *Calvert* v. *Gason*, 2 Sch. & Lef. 561; *Purcell* v. *Nash*, *White* v. *Walsh*, *Lord Waterpark* v. *Austin*, 1 Jon. 625; *Hunt* v. *Browne*, Sa. & Sc. 178; *Prim* v. *Davies*, 1 Hog. 11; *White* v. *Nolan*, 1 Hog. 21; *Crowley* v. *Lord Ely*, 2 Moll. 515.

[8] *Lewis Bowles' Case*, 11 Rep. 82 b; 1 Rol. Rep. 177; Hob. 132.

himself or others during the continuance of his estate.[9]

Term of years without impeachment of waste.

It probably makes no difference whether the estate which is made unimpeachable of waste is freehold or a long term of years determinable on the death of the lessee for life.[1] But where a long term of years unimpeachable of waste is settled on one for life with limitations over, it would seem that the tenant for life is not entitled to waste. Thus,[2] where a wooded property was demised by way of mortgage for 1000 years without impeachment of waste, and the term subsequently became vested in one for life with limitations over, it was declared that the tenant for life was entitled as between herself and the persons claiming in remainder, to cut down and apply for her own benefit such timber as was fit and proper to be cut in the course of a *due and husbandlike* management of the woods in question. This is the right of an ordinary lessee for life of a wooded property, impeachable of waste,[3] a tenant for life

[9] Co. Litt. 220 a; *Pyne* v. *Dor*, 1 T. R. 55. The authorities are collected in a learned note, 2 Swanst. 145.

[1] *Garth* v. *Cotton*, 1 W. & T. Lead. Ca.; 3 Atk. 751; 1 Ves. 524, 546; 1 Dick. 183.

[2] *Bridges* v. *Stephens*, 2 Swanst. 150, *n.*

[3] *Ferrand* v. *Wilson*, 4 Hare, 344.

without impeachment of waste being entitled to do more.[4] There seems indeed to be no reason why the tenant for life of such a term should have larger powers to commit waste than would have belonged to her if the subject of settlement had been the fee.

Tenant for life in remainder.

It is hardly necessary to observe that a tenant for life in remainder without impeachment of waste cannot authorise waste to be committed before his estate has come into possession.[5]

Tenant in tail after possibility.

Tenant in tail after possibility of issue extinct,[6] and tenant in fee simple subject to an executory devise over,[7] are not punishable of waste at law,

[4] *Smythe* v. *Smythe*, 2 Swanst. 251; *Downshire* v. *Sandys*, 6 Ves. 107.

[5] *Lewis Bowles' Case*, 11 Rep. 79; *Lady Evelyn's Case*, 2 Swanst. 172; *Fleming* v. *Bishop of Carlisle* (cited in *Garth* v. *Cotton*), 1 Dick. 209. See, however, *Aspinwall* v. *Leigh*, 2 Vern. 218; 1 Eq. Ab. 400; *Claxton* v. *Claxton*, 2 Vern. 152; *Davies* v. *Davies*, 2 Ir. Eq. R. 415. As to whether timber, &c. wrongfully severed vests in tenant for life in remainder without impeachment of waste, or in a subsequent remainderman of inheritance, see *Gent* v. *Harrison*, J. 517, and post, Sect. 4.

[6] *Skelton* v. *Skelton*, 2 Swanst. 170; *Abrahall* v. *Bubb*, 2 Freem. 53; 2 Show. 69; 2 Eq. Ab. 757; 2 Swanst. 172; *Williams* v. *Williams*, 12 East, 209; 15 Ves. 425; (note Lord Eldon's query); and see ante, p. 6.

[7] *Turner* v. *Wright*, J. 740; on appeal, 2 D. F. & J. 234, reviewing *Robinson* v. *Litton*, 3 Atk. 209; 6 Cru. Dig. 428, 429; Vin. Abr. 475; *Stansfield* v. *Hubergham*, 10 Ves. 273; *Wright*

and seem to be in effect in the same position as tenant for life without impeachment of waste.

Jurisdiction in equity.

"In restraining waste by persons having limited interests in property, the courts of equity have generally proceeded on the ground of the common law rights of the parties, and the difficulty of obtaining immediate preservation of property from destruction or irreparable injury by the process of the common law; but upon this subject the jurisdiction has been extended to cases in which the remedies provided in those courts could not be made to apply."[8] Thus,[9] as early as the time of Richard II., a remainderman in fee obtained an injunction to stay waste by a tenant for life although the existence of an intermediate life estate formed a temporary impediment to the action at law.

No action at law.

Another case in which equity interposes, although no action would lie, is where a person who may be injured by the waste has no remedy at law by reason of the weakness of his estate, as,

v. *Atkyns*, 17 Ves. 255 ; 19 Ves. 299 ; 1 Ves. & B. 313 ; T. & R. 143 ; G. Coop. 111 ; Lord St. Leonards' Law of Property, 376—388.

[8] Mit. Pl., 4th edit. 114.

[9] Moore, 554 ; see 2 Inst. 301.

for example, where there is tenant for life remainder for life with or without impeachment of waste with remainders over, the court will restrain the first tenant for life on the bill of the remainderman for life,[1] even although the remainderman of inheritance may approve of the waste which is being done.[2] So where there was tenant for life remainder to the first son for life without impeachment of waste with remainders over, and the first son by leave of the lessee at will of the father came upon the land and felled trees, although in that case no action of waste or trespass lay, he was enjoined at his father's suit.[3] Again, an injunction to stay waste has been granted on behalf of an infant *en ventre sa mère*.[4] And in the leading case of *Garth* v. *Cotton*,[5] Lord Hardwicke held that trustees to

[1] *Dayrell* v. *Champness*, Eq. Ab. 400; 1 Inst. 53; Cary, 27—36; *Roswell's Case*, 1 Roll. Ab. 377; *Tracy* v. *Tracy*, 1 Vern. 23; *Perrot* v. *Perrot*, 3 Atk. 95.

[2] *Dayrell* v. *Champness* (cited *Garth* v. *Cotton*), 1 Dick. 197, 198; see *Molyneux* v. *Powell*, 3 P. W. 268, *n.*; Eden on Injunctions, 163.

[3] *Lady Evelyn's Case*, 2 Freem. 55; 2 Swanst. 272; see ante, p. 5; *Anon.*, 1 Ves. J. 93.

[4] *Luttrell's Case*, cited *Hale* v. *Hale*, Prec. Ch. 50; 2 Vern. 710; 2 Atk. 117; *Robinson* v. *Litton*, 3 Atk. 209.

[5] 1 Ves. 524, 546; 1 Dick. 183; 3 Atk. 751; 1 W. & T. Lead. Ca.

preserve contingent remainders might have an injunction against a tenant for life and a remote remainderman colluding to commit waste whilst the mesne remainders were in expectancy.

Infant tenant in tail in possession.

Of course no action lies by a remainderman against a tenant in tail in possession committing waste; and it has been decided that where the tenant in tail is an infant, the guardian may commit waste, although by changing the nature of the property from realty to personalty it may, in the event of the infant's death under twenty-one, benefit the next of kin at the remainderman's expense. This was held in *Saville* v. *Saville*,[6] where the guardian was proceeding to cut down a great quantity of timber whilst the infant was in very bad health, so that he died shortly afterwards. It was said that if such an application had been made on behalf of the infant himself the result might have been different.[7] And to the same effect Lord Hardwicke in a subsequent case[8] laid it down,—"An infant tenant in tail has the same right as one of full age as regards the remainder-

[6] Ca. temp. Talbot, 16; 1 Ves. S. 548; Amb. 371; and see 2 Ves. S. 362, and post, Sect. 4.

[7] *Hussey* v. *Hussey*, 5 Madd. 44.

[8] *Lyddal* v. *Clavering*, Amb. 371.

man, though indeed the guardian is solely accountable for his management to the infant at the full age, or to any one who stands in his place."

Feme coverte tenant in tail.

A feme tenant in tail in possession and her husband contracted to sell standing timber. The feme died and the husband who was now become tenant by the curtesie was restrained from cutting the timber on the bill of the infant heir in tail.[9]

Legal estate in trustees.

Where a legal estate is vested in trustees upon trust for a tenant for life with remainders over, and the tenant for life is actively committing waste, the trustees have a right to interfere, and it is their duty to do so if persons unborn are interested.[1] But they have no such right or duty in respect of permissive waste, and are, therefore, not subject to any liability by reason of the tenant for life allowing the premises to get out of repair.[2]

Trustees cutting ornamental timber.

In *Campbell* v. *Allgood*,[3] it was said that trustees

[9] *Roberts* v. *Roberts*, Hard. 96.

[1] *Pugh* v. *Vaughan*, 12 Beav. 517; *Powys* v. *Blagrave*, Kay, 495; 4 D. M. G. 448; see *Denton* v. *Denton*, 7 Beav. 388.

[2] *Powys* v. *Blagrave*, ut sup.; see *Cooke* v. *Cholmondeley*, 4 Jur. N. S. 827; *Warren* v. *Rudall, ex parte Godfrey*, 29 L. J. Ch. 543; 1 J. & H. 1.

[3] 17 Beav. 623.

CHAP. I. Sect. 1.

who cut down ornamental trees without the consent of the parties interested, or the authority of the Court, were bound to show that it was absolutely necessary for the well-being, salubrity, and comfort of the residence that the trees should be so cut.

Copyholds

An injunction for waste will lie by a copyholder against his lessee,[4] by a copyholder in remainder against a copyholder for life,[5] and, according to the later authorities, by a lord of a manor against his copyhold tenants,[6] or their undertenants,[7] and an interlocutory injunction has been granted, although the answer denied that the lands were copyhold.[8]

Tenant in common.

The Statute of Westminster the second gave one tenant in common, or joint tenant, an action against another for acts which would be waste in a tenant for years or tenant for life.[9] It seems

[4] *Dalton* v. *Gill and Pinder*, Cary, 89, 90.

[5] *Cornish* v. *New*, Finch, 220; *Caldwell* v. *Baylis*, 2 Mer. 408; Scriven, 4th edit. p. 426.

[6] *Attorney-General* v. *Vincent*, Bunb. 192; *Dench* v. *Bampton*, 4 Ves. 700; *Richards* v. *Noble*, 3 Mer. 673; *Parrott* v. *Palmer*, 3 My. & K. 639; Mit. Pl., 4th edit. 139; see *Andrews* v. *Hulse*, 4 K. & J. 392.

[7] *Cuddon* v. *Morley*, 7 Hare, 202.

[8] *Commissioners of Greenwich Hospital* v. *Blackett*, 12 Jur. 151.

[9] 2 Inst. 403.

that a parson might restrain waste by one who was tenant in common with him,[1] but formerly such injunctions were in general refused on the ground that the party aggrieved ought to apply for a partition.[2] An injunction will now, however, be granted where the wrong-doer is insolvent,[3] or occupying tenant to the other,[4] or where the waste is of a very aggravated character, amounting to destruction.[5]

Sect. 2.—EQUITABLE WASTE.

Sect. 2.

Tenant for life without impeachment of waste.

A VERY remarkable instance of the interference of a court of equity to stay waste, where no action would lie, is where a tenant for life, without impeachment of waste, is restrained from exercising his legal power. If such a tenant is committing acts of a character especially destructive to the inheritance, or still more, acts of

[1] 2 Inst. 403 ; *Liford's Case*, 11 Rep. 46.

[2] *Goodwyn* v. *Spray*, 2 Dick. 667.

[3] *Smallman* v. *Onions*, 3 Bro. C. C. 620

[4] *Twort* v. *Twort*, 16 Ves. 128 ; see Moore, 71, pl. 194.

[5] *Hole* v. *Thomas*, 7 Ves. 589; *Durham Co.* v. *Wawn*, 3 Beav. 119 ; 2 Railw. Ca. 395 ; and see *Jeffrey* v. *Smith*, 1 J. & W. 298 ; *Frazer* v. *Kershaw*, 2 K. & J. 496.

CHAP. I. Sect. 2.

wanton or malicious mischief, the Court holds that his legal power to commit waste is being used unconscientiously, and has assumed jurisdiction to restrain him.[6] The aggravated acts of waste which fall within this principle are termed Equitable waste. The most important of them are, (1) Pulling down the mansion-house,[7] or other houses or buildings on the estate;[8] (2) Felling ornamental or very young trees,[9] or destroying underwood.[1]

It has been said that the jurisdiction is to be considered as founded on a breach of trust reposed in the tenant for life, that he will use his legal estate only for the purpose of fair enjoyment.[2] But this mode of expressing the doctrine has met with disapproval.[3]

[6] Mit. Pl., 4th edit. p. 140; *Micklethwaite* v. *Micklethwaite*, 1 D. & J. 524.

[7] *Vane* v. *Barnard*, 2 Vern. 738; Prec. Ch. 454; Gilb. Eq. Rep. 127; 1 Eq. Ab. 399; 1 Salk. 161.

[8] *Aston* v. *Aston*, 1 Ves. S. 265; *Rolt* v. *Somerville*, 2 Eq. Ab. 759.

[9] *Chamberlayne* v. *Dummer*, 1 Bro. C. C. 166; 3 Bro. C. C. 548.

[1] *Aston* v. *Aston*, 1 Ves. 265; *Brydges* v. *Stephens*, 6 Madd. 279.

[2] *Ormonde* v. *Kynersley*, 5 Madd. 369.

[3] *Kingham* v. *Lee*, 15 Sim. 399; *Powys* v. *Blagrave*, Kay, 501; 4 D. M. G. 448. It seems to have escaped notice that

CHAP. I.

Sect. 2.

Other persons within the same principle.

Tenant in tail after possibility of issue extinct,[4] tenant in fee with an executory devise over,[5] and an heir taking by resulting trust until the happening of a contingency,[6] are within the principle of equitable waste; but a tenant in tail restrained by statute from barring his issue and those in remainder is not.[7]

Sect. 3.—GENERAL MATTERS RELATING TO WASTE.

Sect. 3.

ccount.

WHEN the legal owner of the things severed comes into equity to stay future waste, he may at the same time have an account of past waste, in order to prevent multiplicity of suits;[8] but

Ormonde v. *Kynersley*, was ultimately reversed, 7 L. J. Ch. 150; 8 L. J. Ch. 67, and post, p. 46.

[4] *Abrahall* v. *Bubb*, 2 Freem. 53; 2 Eq. Ab. 757; 2 Show. 69; 2 Swanst. 172; *Garth* v. *Cotton*, 1 W. & T. Lead. Ca.; *Cook* v. *Whalley*, 1 Eq. Ab. 400; *Williams* v. *Day*, 2 Ch. Ca. 32; Prec. Ch. 454.

[5] *Turner* v. *Wright*, J. 740; on appeal, 2 D. F. & J. 234.

[6] *Stansfield* v. *Habergham*, 10 Ves. 278.

[7] *Attorney-General* v. *Duke of Marlborough*, 3 Mad. 498; *Davis* v. *Duke of Marlborough*, 2 Swanst. 108.

[8] *Whitfield* v. *Bewit*, 2 P. W. 240; *Jesus College* v. *Bloom*, 1 Amb. 54; 3 Atk. 262; *Lee* v. *Alston*, 1 Bro. C. C. 194; 3 Bro. C. C. 37; 1 Ves. J. 78; *Parrot* v. *Palmer*, 3 M. & K. 632; *Richards* v. *Noble*, 3 Mer. 673.

Chap. 1.
Sect. 3.

where, from the determination of the estate of the wrong-doer, or some other such reason, there is nothing on which the injunction could operate, and complete relief may be obtained in an action at law, as a general rule a bill for an account will not lie.[9] Mines are an exception to this rule, because they are a species of trade.[1] A person, however, suing in respect of the equitable property only in the things severed, may have an account wholly irrespective of an injunction.[2]

Remainderman life.

A mesne remainderman for life, although entitled to an injunction to protect his enjoyment, has no interest to call for an account.[3]

In an action of trover, damages are recovered

[9] *Jesus College* v. *Bloom*, 1 Amb. 54; 3 Atk. 262; *Smith* v. *Cooke*, 3 Atk. 381; *Parrot* v. *Palmer*, 3 M. & K. 642; *Pulteney* v. *Warren*, 6 Ves. 89; *Grierson* v. *Eyre*, 9 Ves. 346; *Gent* v. *Harrison*, J. 521; see *Fishmongers' Co.* v. *Beresford*, Beat. 613; *Lee* v. *Alston*, ut sup.

[1] *Bishop of Winchester* v. *Knight*, 1 P. W. 406; 2 Eq. Ab. 226, pl. 7; *Jesus College* v. *Bloom*, 1 Amb. 54; 3 Atk. 262; *Story* v. *Windsor*, 2 Atk. 630; *Jeffery* v. *Smith*, 1 J. & W. 298; see *Thomas* v. *Oakley*, 18 Ves. 184.

[2] *Garth* v. *Cotton*, 3 Atk. 751; 1 Ves. S. 524, 546; 1 Dick. 183; 1 W. & T. Lead. Ca.; *Lansdowne* v. *Lansdowne*, 1 Mad. 116; *Duke of Leeds* v. *Earl Amherst*, 2 Phil. 117; 16 Sim. 431; *Morris* v. *Morris*, 3 D. & J. 323, and many other cases.

[3] *Pigott* v. *Bullock*, 3 Bro. C. C. 538; 1 Ves. J. 479.

for the waste done; but in a suit in equity, the account taken is of the produce only.[4]

Statute of Limitations.

If a tenant for life has within six years rendered accounts to the remainderman of timber, &c., severed during a period ending more than six years before a bill is filed for an account of such timber, &c., and the value of it, the Statute of Limitations cannot be pleaded to the bill.[5]

Delay.

A bill will in general lie against an executor for an account of waste committed by his testator;[6] but where the waste had been committed during forty-three years preceding the tenant's decease, and the bill was not filed until six years after, the account was refused on the ground of delay as to all the waste in his lifetime, but granted with an injunction as to waste by the executors.[7]

When application for an in-

It is not necessary to wait before applying for

[4] *Lee* v. *Alston*, 1 Bro. C. C. 194; 3 Bro. C. C. 37; 1 Ves. J. 78; *Morris* v. *Morris*, 3 D. & J. 323; see *Brown* v. *Lady Bridges*, Toth. 114; *Powell* v. *Aiken*, 4 K. & J. 351; 21 & 22 Vict. c. 27, sect. 2.

[5] *Hony* v. *Hony*, 1 S. & S. 568.

[6] *Bishop of Winchester* v. *Knight*, 1 P. W. 407; *Lansdowne* v. *Lansdowne*, 1 Mad. 116; *Thomas* v. *Oakley*, 18 Ves. 186; see *Hambly* v. *Trott*, Cowp. 376; 3 & 4 Will. 4, c. 42, § 2.

[7] *Fishmongers' Co.* v. *Beresford*, Beat. 613; *Harcourt* v. *White*, 6 Jur. N. S. 1087.

CHAP. I.
Sect. 3.
junction should be made.

an injunction until a serious act of waste has been committed; it is sufficient if waste is done only in a slight degree, manifesting an intent to do more, or if it is merely threatened;[8] and delay is not so prejudicial to the plaintiff in cases of waste, as in other applications for injunctions.[9] Hearsay evidence is admitted on an interlocutory application.[1]

Parties.

The remainderman of an undivided share of the inheritance may have an injunction and an account.[2]

Where a tenant for life made a lease of coal-mines of such a character as to amount to a forfeiture of his estate, it was held that he could not join with the remainderman in a bill to restrain the lessee from working them.[3]

A bill by a remainderman in tail of two estates, who was also a remainderman for life of a third estate, and the remainderman in tail of this estate joined as co-plaintiff against the tenant for

[8] Barn. Cha. 497; 2 Atk. 183; 3 Atk. 216, 485; *Coffin* v. *Coffin*, Jac. 71; *Barry* v. *Barry*, 1 J. & W. 651.

[9] *Attorney-General* v. *Eastlake*, 11 Hare, 228.

[1] *Beere* v. *Head*, 7 Ir. Eq. 60.

[2] Co. Litt. 53 b; *Whitfield* v. *Bewit*, 2 P. W. 241.

[3] *Wentworth* v. *Turner*, 3 Ves. 3.

life, without impeachment of waste of the three estates, which formed one tract of lands, to restrain cutting ornamental timber, and for an account according to the respective titles, was held not to be multifarious.[4]

Where there is a case for an injunction to stay waste, and the injunction will operate for the benefit of parties not before the Court, notwithstanding a demurrer grounded on the absence of these parties, the Court will interpose.[5]

Lord Hardwicke laid down the rule, that the forfeiture for waste and all penalties ought to be waived in a bill for restraining waste.[6]

An injunction and an account will lie for meliorating waste,[7] but not in general for permissive waste.[8]

[4] *Kingston* v. *Kingston*, 2 Moll. 412.

[5] *Const* v. *Harris*, T. & R. 514.

[6] 1 Atk. 450 ; Mit. Pl., 4th edit. p. 139.

[7] *Brydges* v. *Kilburn*, 5 Ves. 689 ; *Barry* v. *Barry*, 1 J. & W. 651 ; *Duke of Leeds* v. *Earl Amherst*, 2 Phil. 117 ; *Smyth* v. *Carter*, 18 Beav. 78 ; *Morris* v. *Morris*, 3 D. & J. 323 ; *Coppinger* v. *Gubbins*, 3 J. & L. 397 ; 9 Ir. Eq. 304 ; *Molineux* v. *Powell*, 3 P. W. 268 *n.* ; *Doran* v. *Carroll*, 11 Ir. C. L. 379 ; *Simmons* v. *Norton*, 7 Bing. 648.

[8] See post, Sect. 6, Waste in Buildings.

Sect. 4.—WASTE IN TIMBER AND OTHER TREES AND UNDERWOOD.

What is timber.

OAK, ash, and elm are timber in all places, and other trees by the custom of particular counties;[9] thus,[1] birch trees are considered to be timber in Yorkshire and Cumberland; beech, cherry, and aspen in Buckinghamshire; beech also in Gloucestershire and Bedfordshire; beech and willows in Hants. In some places whitethorn, holly, blackthorn, horse-chesnut, lime, yew, walnut, crab, and hornbeam; in other districts pollards, or other timber trees which have been lopped, are, contrary to general estimation, also considered timber. It appears that a tree, to be considered timber for the purpose of exemption from tithe, must have attained the age of twenty years, whatever its solid contents or other qualifications may be.[2]

[9] Co. Litt. 53 a.

[1] Cru. Dig., 4th edit. tit. III. chap. II. sec. 7; *Barrett* v. *Barrett*, Het. 36; *Bullen* v. *Denning*, 5 B. & C. 842; *Duke of Chandos* v. *Talbot*, 2 P. W. 606; see *Gordon* v. *Woodford*, 6 Jur. N. S. 59.

[2] 2 Inst. 643; *Aubrey* v. *Fisher*, 10 East, 446; see *Chamberlayne* v. *Dummer*, 3 Bro. C. C. 549; *Smythe* v. *Smythe*, 2 Swanst. 252.

CHAP. I.
Sect. 4.
Property in growing trees, &c.

The general property[3] of timber trees is in the lessor, who has the inheritance of the land, but the lessee for life or years has a special interest and property in the fruit and shade[4] so long as they are annexed, so that if a man cut down timber trees, the lessee shall have trespass. Moreover, the lessee has a general property in hedges, bushes, trees, &c., which are not timber,[5] and he may cut or lop them for his own benefit in a reasonable manner, but not so as to prevent the future growth.[6]

Even if the lease be of lands, trees, &c., expressly mentioning the trees, this does not give the lessee a right to fell them.[7]

Copyholder.

A copyholder being considered to be a tenant at will, has in general the same possessory interest in the trees as a lessee of freeholds, the property being in the lord. But by custom

[3] Com. Dig. 'Biens' (H); 11 Rep. 48; *Herring* v. *Dean and Chapter of St. Paul's*, 3 Swanst. 492; *Berriman* v. *Peacock*, 9 Bing. 384; *Alexander* v. *Godley*, 6 Ir. C. L. 458.

[4] 4 Rep. 62 b; Dy. 90; 1 Rol. 181.

[5] 4 Rep. 62; 1 Rol. 181.

[6] 2 Rol. Abr. 815; Co. Litt. 53 a; Hob. 219; *Pidgeley* v. *Rawling*, 2 Coll. 275.

[7] *Herring* v. *Dean and Chapter of St. Paul's*, 3 Swanst. 512; citing *Liford's Case*, 11 Rep. 46 b; Dy. 374, pl. 18; Shepherd's Touch. 95.

Chap. I.
Sect. 4.

the proprietary right may be attached to a copyhold of inheritance, or to a copyhold for life, with power to renew or nominate a successor.[8]

The lessee a nurseryman.

A nurseryman who plants fruit or other trees for the purpose of his trade, may remove them during, or at the expiration of the term of his lease, provided they have not become of larger growth than could be dealt with by him in the ordinary way of his trade.[9]

Waste in trees, &c.

"The[1] destruction of germens or young plants destined to become trees,[2] which destroys the future timber, is waste; the cutting of apple-trees in a garden or orchard, or the cutting down a hedge of thorns,[3] which changes the nature of the thing demised, or the eradicating or unseasonable cutting of whitethorns,[4] which destroys the future growth, are all acts of waste. On the other hand, those acts are not waste which are not prejudicial to the inheritance,[5] as

[8] Scriven, 4th edit. p. 419; *Jefferson* v. *Jefferson*, 3 Lev. 131.

[9] *Wardell* v. *Usher*, 3 Sc. N. R. 508.

[1] *Phillips* v. *Smith*, 14 M. & W. 589.

[2] Co. Litt. 43.

[3] Co. Litt. 53 a.

[4] Vin. Abr. 'Waste' (E).

[5] *Barret* v. *Barret*, Het. 36.

the cutting of sallows, maples, beeches, and thorns, alleged to be of the age of thirty-three years, but not timber either by general law or particular local custom. So likewise the cutting even of oaks or ashes where they are of seasonable wood, *i. e.*, where they are cut usually as underwood, and in due course are to grow up again from the stumps, is not waste. Now, if we apply the principles to be extracted from all these authorities to the present case, we have no difficulty in saying that the cutting of these willows does not amount to waste. They are not timber-trees, and when cut down they are not, so far as appears by the evidence, destroyed, but grow up again from their stumps, and produce again their ordinary and usual profit from such growth; therefore, neither is the thing demised destroyed, nor is the thing demised changed as to the inheritance, for profit remains as before, derivable from the reproduction of the wood from the stumps of the willows cut down. Nor are the trees in such a situation as to make the cutting of them waste, by what is called collateral respect, as where trees not timber are situated so as to become useful for the protection of a house,[6] and so become as it were a part of the house, as in Hob. 219, willows growing within the site of a house. Nor are they willows within view of the manor house, which defend it from the wind, or in a bank to sustain a bank (12 H. 81), or like whitethorns used for the like purposes, or where they stand in a field depastured, and are used for the shade of the beasts depasturing, and so are intended permanently to remain in that particular form, for the advantage of those to whom the inheritance may thereafter come."

Estovers.

A tenant may take sufficient wood to repair the walls, pales, fences, hedges, and ditches as he found them, and he may also take for agricultural and household purposes what is known as plowbote, firebote, and housebote.[7] Such cuttings are commonly called estovers, and are justifiable, or not, according to the application made of them, and to whether they are or are not of utility to the estate on which they are cut. Thus, estovers cut on one estate, cannot be applied to the repairs on another;[8] and a tenant

[6] Co. Litt. 53.

[7] Co. Litt. 53 b.

[8] *Lee* v. *Alston*, 1 Bro. C. C. 167; 3 Bro. C. C. 37; 1 Ves. J. 78; *Nash* v. *Earl of Derby*, 2 Vern. 537.

may not sell wood to form a fund for defraying the expense of past or contemplated repairs, or exchange it for other wood more fit; even if he buys the same wood back again, it is waste.[9]

In *Cole* v. *Peyson*,[1] a tenant for life was restrained from cutting good timber trees for fuel; it appears, however, that a lessee may cut timber for the repair of the house,[2] and under some circumstances when it impedes the growth of underwood.[3]

A copyholder is entitled to estovers by custom, and possibly without.[4]

Property in severed timber.

When timber is severed accidentally,[5] as by tempest, or is wrongfully cut down by a person having a limited interest, or by a mere trespasser, it belongs to him who has the first estate of inheritance, and he may bring trover

[9] Co. Litt. 53 b; *Simmons* v. *Morton*, 7 Bing. 640; *Whitfield* v. *Bewit*, 2 P. W. 241; post, Sect. 9; Eden on Injunctions, p. 147; Cru. Dig. 'Estate for Life.'

[1] Ch. Rep. 106.

[2] Eden on Injunctions, p. 146.

[3] *Knight* v. *Duplessis*, 2 Ves. S. 360, 555; 16 Ves. 179.

[4] Scriven, 'Copyholds,' 4th edit. p. 419.

[5] *Duke of Newcastle* v. *Vane*, 2 P. W. 241; *Garth* v. *Cotton*, 1 W. & T. Lead. Ca.; 1 Ves. 524, 546; 3 Atk. 751; 1 Dick. 183; *Lee* v. *Alston*, 1 Bro. C. C. 196; *Bewick* v. *Whitfield*, 3 P. W. 268; see *Lushington* v. *Boldero*, 15 Beav. 7.

for it, or recover the sum for which it has been sold.[6]

In *Gent* v. *Harrison*,[7] a vested estate for life without impeachment of waste was interposed between the estate in possession, which was impeachable of waste, and the first estate of inheritance. The tenant in possession having wrongfully cut timber, it was contended that the property vested in the owner of the estate for life in remainder without impeachment of waste, and not in the owner of the inheritance. Wood, V.C., inclined strongly to the contrary opinion, but the point did not call for decision. And to the same effect seems *Piggot* v. *Bullock*,[8] where underwood which was cut for sale by a tenant for life, who was under an express restriction from so cutting, was held to vest in the owner of the inheritance and not in a subsequent tenant for life.

[6] 4 Rep. 62 a; 5 Rep. 76 b; 11 Rep. 46; *Lewis Bowles' Case*, 11 Rep. 79; 1 Rol. 177; 3 Lev. 209; *Berry* v. *Heard*, Cro. Car. 242; W. Jones, 255; *Udal* v. *Udal*, Al. 81; *Whitfield* v. *Bewit*, 2 P. W. 240; *Williams* v. *Duke of Bolton*, 3 P. W. 268; *Powlett* v. *Duchess of Bolton*, 3 Ves. 374; *Dare* v. *Hopkins*, 2 Cox, 110; *Gent* v. *Harrison*, J. 524.

[7] J. 517; see 1 Ves. J. 484; and as to timber rightfully cut, *Waldo* v. *Waldo*, 12 Sim. 107; *Phillips* v. *Barlow*, 14 Sim. 263.

[8] 1 Ves. J. 479.

Copyholds.

When timber trees on copyhold land are separated from the soil by whatever act or casualty, in the absence of special custom, the tenant's possessory right ends, and the lord may take them. But as to pollards, dotards, bushes, &c., the law is otherwise; and if thrown down, they belong to the tenant.[9]

Remainderman not allowed to benefit by his own wrong.

In the common case of a family settlement, where there is a tenant for life with remainder to his children successively in tail with remainders over, the owner of the first estate of inheritance, before any children are born, may be a remote relation who has little chance of ever succeeding to the estate. Although equity will not prevent such a remainderman from enjoying the benefit of the rule of law where he has not been a party to the waste, he will not be permitted to join with the tenant in possession in committing waste for their common benefit. This was decided in *Garth* v. *Cotton*.[1] There Mr. Garth, the plaintiff's father, was tenant for 99 years, if he should so long live, impeachable of voluntary

[9] Com. Dig. 'Biens' (H); Scriven, 4th edit. p. 422, n. (*j*), and authorities there cited, which see also as to trees not timber.

[1] 3 Atk. 751; 1 Ves. 524, 546; 1 Dick. 183; 1 W. & T. Lead. Ca.

Chap. 1. Sect. 4.

waste,[2] with remainder to trustees to preserve contingent remainders, with remainder to his first and every other son in tail, with the remainder to the defendant in fee. Before Mr. Garth had any children he entered into an agreement with the defendant to cut down timber and divide the profits between them. Afterwards he had a son born, who, after his father's death, succeeded in compelling the defendant to refund his share of the timber money.

In *Williams* v. *Duke of Bolton*,[3] the tenant for life doing waste had himself the next estate of inheritance. The facts were that the Duke was tenant for life with contingent remainders to his first and other sons in tail, with remainder to Mrs. Orde for life, with remainder to her first and other sons in tail, with remainders over, with remainder to the Duke in fee. There were trustees to preserve all the contingent remainders. The Duke cut timber whilst the contingent estates were in expectancy. Lord Thurlow was of opinion that although the Duke had a vested remainder, yet as it was not competent for him to

[2] *Vincent* v. *Spicer*, 22 Beav. 380.
[3] 1 Cox, 72 ; 3 P. W. 268.

cut down the timber in respect of his life estate, he could not take advantage in respect of his estate in remainder of his own wrong, and he was ordered to pay the value into court. In a subsequent suit[4] after the Duke's death, the money was directed to be laid out in land to be settled to the uses of the estate on which the timber was cut.

Tenant for life without impeachment not permitted to derive advantage from sales or exchanges.

So also a tenant for life without impeachment of waste will not be permitted to derive an undue advantage from the exercise of a power or trust for sale, or exchange of the settled estates. Thus in *Lady Plymouth* v. *Archer*,[5] land was devised upon trust for sale, the produce to be invested in other lands, which when purchased were to be to the use of Lord Archer for life without impeachment of waste, with remainders over: and there was a declaration that the rents and profits of the lands until sold were to be to the use of the same persons who would be entitled to the lands to be purchased. Lord Archer was not allowed to cut timber upon the estate to be sold,

[4] *Powlett* v. *Duchess of Bolton*, 3 Ves. 374 ; see *Dare* v. *Hopkins*, 2 Cox, 110.

[5] 1 Bro. C. C. 159 ; *Wolf* v. *Hill*, 2 Swanst. 149.

CHAP. I. Sect. 4.

because, as he would have a right to cut timber upon the estate to be bought, that would be to give him double waste. In a case [6] before Lord Eldon, trustees for the purchase of real estate were made successively tenants for life without impeachment of waste of the estate to be purchased. His lordship said, "If the timber bear a very considerable proportion to the value of the whole purchase, the tenant for life, especially as he is one of the trustees, cannot possibly be permitted to take it. The Court may be driven to take this course; that trustees laying out the fund in a timbered estate without applying that reasonable and discreet attention, that in a fair view ought to be applied to the interests of all parties, should be considered in a court of equity as not buying any timber for their own benefit." And where trustees are selling under a power of sale, a tenant for life without impeachment of waste is not entitled to the price of the timber.[7]

Equitable waste in trees, &c.

The principle upon which a tenant for life without impeachment of waste is restrained from

[6] *Burges* v. *Lamb*, 16 Ves. 174.

[7] *Wolf* v. *Hill*, 2 Swanst. 149 *n.*; *Doran* v. *Wiltshire*, 3 Swanst. 699; *Cholmeley* v. *Paxton*, 3 Bing. 207; 5 Bing. 48; 3 Russ. 565; 2 Moore & Payne, 127; 10 B. & C. 564; nom. *Cockerell*

cutting ornamental timber is thus stated[8] by Turner, L. J.: "If a devisor or settlor occupies a mansion house with trees[9] planted or left standing for ornament around or about it, or keeps such a mansion house in a state for occupation, and devises it or settles it so as to go in a course of succession, he may reasonably be presumed to anticipate that those who are to succeed him will occupy the mansion house; and it cannot be presumed that he meant it to be denuded of that ornament which he has himself enjoyed."[1]

Settlor tenant for life.

And it appears that if an owner in fee settles the estate on himself for life with remainders over, he will not be allowed any larger privileges

v. *Cholmeley*, 1 Russ. & Myl. 418; 1 Cl. & F. 60; Sug. H.L. C. 491; Lord St. Leonards' Powers, 8th edit. p. 864; see 22 & 23 Vict. c. 35, s. 13.

[8] *Micklethwaite* v. *Micklethwaite*, 1 D. & J. 524; see *Marker* v. *Marker*, 9 Hare, 1.

[9] The distinction between timber and other trees does not seem to be material; see Common Order, Seton on Decrees.

[1] In addition to the cases on this subject elsewhere referred to, the reader may consult *Abrahall* v. *Bubb*, Freem. Rep. 53; 2 Swanst. 172; 2 Eq. Ab. 757; *Bishop of Winchester's Case* and *Lady Elevyn's Case*, 2 Eq. Ab. 757; *Anon.*, Freem. Rep. 278; 2 Eq. Ab. 758; *Rolt* v. *Somerville*, 2 Eq. Ab. 759; *Kaye* v. *Banks*, Dick. 431; *Leighton* v. *Leighton*, 1 Bro. C. C. 168; *O'Brien* v. *O'Brien*, Amb. 107; *Chamberlayne* v. *Dummer*, 1 Bro. C. C. 166; 3 Bro. C. C. 549; *Williams* v. *M'Namara*, 8 Ves. 70; *Lawley* v. *Lawley*, Jac. 71 *n.*; *Lansdowne* v. *Lansdowne*, 1 Mad. 116.

CHAP. 1.
Sect. 4.

than he would have had if the settlor had been a stranger,[2] and consequently he will not be permitted to cut timber planted by himself for ornament before the date of the settlement.[3]

Trees must be connected with mansion house.

Trees to be protected under this principle must be connected with a mansion house;[4] they need not, however, be in immediate proximity to it[5] if they form part of any avenue or vista; and in a case[6] which has perhaps gone farther than any other, Lord Eldon protected clumps and rows of firs which were planted for ornament on a common, at a distance of at least two miles from the house, and separated from it by the land of other owners, the reason appearing to be that they were connected with a drive. A tenant for life, however, cannot entitle himself to cut ornamental timber by pulling down the house wrong-

[2] *Vincent* v. *Spicer*, 22 Beav. 380; *Vane* v. *Barnard*, 2 Vern. 738; Prec. Ch. 454; *Barry* v. *Barry*, 1 J. & W. 652.

[3] The author so understauds the dictum in *Coffin* v. *Coffin*, Jac. 71; but this and a similar dictum of Lord Erskine in ——— v. *Copley*, 1 Mad. Ch. Pr. 200; 3 Mad. Rep. 525; may possibly be referred to trees planted by a tenant for life after the settlement; see, however, *Piers* v. *Piers*, 1 Ves. S. 521.

[4] *Micklethwaite* v. *Micklethwaite*, 1 D. & J. 504.

[5] *Strathmore* v. *Bowes*, 2 Bro. C. C. 88; *Packington's Case*, 3 Atk. 215; *Charlton's Case*, there cited.

[6] *Downshire* v. *Sandys*, 6 Ves. 110; see *Wombwell* v. *Bellasyse*, 6 Ves. 110 b; *Burges* v. *Lamb*, 16 Ves. 174.

fully, or by taking it down rightfully, if the settlement contemplates that it should be rebuilt, or that the grounds should be let on building leases.[7] But where a house which had formerly been a principal mansion house, but had gone to decay, was restored by the tenant for life, this was held not to give protection, as against him, to the timber about it.[8]

A ride through a wood.

A ride cut through a wood will not protect more than is necessary for the purposes of the ride.[9]

What trees are ornamental.

Trees are treated as ornamental if they have been planted or left standing for ornament by the settlor, but not otherwise; so that a subsequent owner will not be allowed to fell such trees, however distasteful their appearance may be to him, and on the other hand, trees ornamental in fact will not be protected unless the settlor dedicated them to the purpose of ornament.[1] But, "If a

[7] *Wellesley* v. *Wellesley*, 6 Sim. 497; *Morris* v. *Morris*, 15 Sim. 505; 11 Jur. 196; 3 D. & J. 323; *Micklethwaite* v. *Micklethwaite*, 1 D. & J. 529.

[8] *Newdigate* v. *Newdigate*, 8 Bli. N S. 734; 1 Sim. 131; 2 Cl. & F. 601.

[9] *Wombwell* v. *Bellasyse*, 6 Ves. 110 a; *Burges* v. *Lamb*, 16 Ves. 183; *Halliwell* v. *Phillips*, 6 W. R. 408; 4 Jur. N. S. 607.

[1] *Downshire* v. *Sandys*, 6 Ves. 110; *Wombwell* v. *Bellasyse*, 6 Ves. 110 a; *Mahon* v. *Stanhope*, 3 Mad. 523 *n.*; *Coffin* v. *Coffin*, Jac. 70; *Marker* v. *Marker*, 9 Hare, 17.

CHAP. I.
Sect. 4.

tempest has produced gaps in a piece of ornamental planting, by which unequal and discordant breaks and divisions are occasioned, it would be going too far to hold that cutting a few trees to produce an uniform and consistent, instead of an unpleasant and disjointed effect, should be considered waste."[2] And although the Court will in general abstain from exercising a judgment upon matters of taste, yet where[3] a deed of settlement provided that enough of the most ornamental timber should always remain to leave the beauty of the place unimpaired,[4] Turner, V.C., held that an inquiry might be had whether certain trees could be cut without impairing the beauty of the place as it stood at the date of the settlement.

Preserving for ornament.

It has been justly said,[5] that the fact of planting for ornament is capable of being easily ascer-

[2] *Mahon* v. *Stanhope*, 3 Mad. 523 *n.*; *Lushington* v. *Boldero*, 6 Mad. 149; ——— v. *Copley*, 3 Mad. 525; 1 Mad. Ch. Pr. 200.

[3] *Marker* v. *Marker*, 9 Hare, 1; see *Mann* v. *Stephens*, 15 Sim. 379; *Tulk* v. *Moxhay*, 11 Beav. 571; 2 Phil. 774; 1 H. & T. 105.

[4] See, as to other special clauses, *Chamberlayne* v. *Dummer*, 1 Bro. C. C. 166; 3 Bro. C. C. 548; *Garth* v. *Cotton*, 1 W. & T. Lead. Ca.; *Newdigate* v. *Newdigate*, 1 Sim. 131; *Vincent* v. *Spicer*, 22 Beav. 380.

[5] *Lushington* v. *Boldero*, 6 Mad. 149; see *Halliwell* v. *Phillips*, 6 W. R. 408; 4 Jur. N. S. 607.

tained, but the fact of preserving for ornament is less obvious, and is to be collected from the conduct of the settlor. The leaving trees standing beyond the usual and provident period of cutting, the cleaning out of trees, and surrounding them with pleasure walks and seats, and other circumstances from which an inference arises that the settlor regarded the trees with other views than as mere subjects of profit, are to be considered as *primâ facie* evidence, that trees were left standing for ornament, and more especially when actually connected with that object from their situation. It is doubtful whether the Court can ever go back beyond the time of an absolute owner of the estate for the purpose of ascertaining whether timber is to be treated as ornamental.[6]

rees planted or left standing for shelter, or to exclude objects from view.

The same principles apply to trees planted or left standing for shelter to the mansion house,[7] or for the purpose of excluding objects from view.[8] In the case[9] of a house on the coast of Devonshire,

[6] *Micklethwaite* v. *Micklethwaite*, 1 D. & J. 513.

[7] *Micklethwaite* v. *Micklethwaite*, 1 D. & J. 514 ; and most of the previous cases. Seton on Decrees.

[8] *Day* v. *Merry*, 16 Ves. 375.

[9] *Coffin* v. *Coffin*, Jac. 70.

CHAP. I. Sect. 4.

there were added to the usual form of injunction the words "or which in any manner protected the same from the effects of the sea." But this clause was struck out on appeal as going too far. Possibly legitimate protection from the effects of the sea would be included in the term shelter.

Immature trees.

A tenant for life without impeachment of waste may fell anything which is timber, but not saplings and young trees not fit to be cut for the purposes of timber.[1] In *Smythe* v. *Smythe*,[2] Lord Eldon said, "A tenant for life without impeachment of waste is clearly not compellable to cut timber in such way as a tenant in fee would think most advantageous, but is entitled to cut down anything that is timber. This motion requires an affidavit pledging the deponent that the trees about to be cut are not fit for timber. It is settled that a

How a tenant for life without impeachment of waste may cut.

[1] *Packington's Case*, 3 Atk. 216; *Aston* v. *Aston*, 1 Ves. S. 266; *O'Brien* v. *O'Brien*, 1 Amb. 107; 1 Bro. C. C. 167; *Chamberlayne* v. *Dummer*, 1 Bro. C. C. 166; 3 Bro. C. C. 549; *Strathmore* v. *Bowes*, 2 Bro. C. C. 88; *Tamworth* v. *Ferrers*, 6 Ves. 419; *Potts* v. *Potts*, 3 L. J. Ch. 176.

[2] 2 Swanst. 252; *Coffin* v. *Coffin*, Jac. 72. Lord Eldon at an earlier period seems to have placed a greater restriction on the tenant for life, *Tamworth* v. *Ferrers*, 6 Ves. 420; and see *Pentland* v. *Somerville*, 2 Ir. Ch. 289.

tree which a tenant in fee acting in a husband-like manner would not cut, may be cut by a tenant for life unimpeachable of waste, provided that it is fit for the purpose of timber. A tenant for life unimpeachable of waste might cut down all these trees without question at law; and to subject him in this Court to the rules which a tenant in fee might observe, for the purpose of husbandlike cultivation, would deprive him of almost all his legal rights. If the trees are so far advanced as to become timber the tenant may cut them down though they are in a state to thrive, and though cutting them down would injure the saplings. It is not sufficient to state that this is thriving wood and fit for the purposes of timber. I cannot determine whether a tree measuring less than nine cubic feet is or is not fit for purposes of timber. If the plaintiff files an affidavit, stating that trees measuring less than nine cubic feet are not fit for the purposes of timber, that must be met."[3]

Tenant for life of a term of years without impeachment of waste.

In *Bridges* v. *Stephens*,[4] a lady having a life interest in a mortgage term of 1000 years without

[3] See *Aubrey* v. *Fisher*, 10 East, 446.

[4] 2 Swanst. 150 *n.*; see ante, p. 8.

Chap. I. Sect. 4.

impeachment of waste, was held to be entitled as between herself and the persons claiming in remainder to cut down and apply for her own benefit such timber as was fit and proper to be cut in the course of a due and husbandlike management. As it was a wooded property, this appears to be the right of an ordinary tenant for life impeachable of waste.[5]

Trustees of a term without impeachment of waste.

Trustees of a term without impeachment of waste are bound to a more provident execution of their powers than tenants for life are, and will in general not be allowed to cut timber.[6]

Underwood.

In *Brydges* v. *Stephens*,[7] it was said that upon the same principle on which the Court restrained the cutting of timber of insufficient growth, it would restrain the cutting of underwood not of sufficient growth, according to the custom of the country.

A tenant for life impeachable of waste may not fell even trees which are over ripe and decaying,[8] but as it is for the benefit of all parties interested

[5] *Ferrand* v. *Wilson*, 4 Hare, 344.
[6] *Downshire* v. *Sandys*, 6 Ves. 115.
[7] 6 Mad. 279.
[8] *Perrot* v. *Perrot*, 3 Atk. 95 ; see now 19 & 20 Vict. c. 120, s. 11.

Decaying timber.

in the estate that such timber should be cut and sold, the Court of Chancery has from an early period given authority to do so, and directed a proper application of the proceeds. Timber felled under the direction of the Court, or in such manner as the Court approves,[9] is said to be rightfully cut.

Application of fund produced by timber (not ornamental) rightfully cut.

In an early case[1] of this nature it was held that the tenant for life should not have any share of the money arising from the sale of the timber, but that care was to be taken to leave enough timber on the estate for repairs and botes, and that whatever damage was done to him on the premises should be made good. In another case,[2] occurring about the same time, A. was tenant for life with remainder to trustees, to preserve, &c., remainder to C. (the plaintiff) in tail with remainder over, with power for A., with the consent of the trustees, to fell timber, and the money arising therefrom was to be invested in land, to the same uses, &c. A. felled timber to the value of 3000*l.* without the consent of the trustees, who never intermeddled.

[9] *Waldo* v. *Waldo*, 12 Sim. 107.

[1] *Bewick* v. *Whitfield*, 3 P. W. 268.

[2] *Castlemaine* v. *Craven*, 2 Eq. Ab. 758 ; 22 Vin. Abr. 523.

Chap. I.
Sect. 4.

C. asked for an injunction and account. His honour (Sir J. Jekyll) said that the timber might be considered under two denominations, to wit, such as was thriving and not fit to be felled, and such as was unthriving and what a prudent man and a good husband would fell, &c. And the value of the former was to go as waste to the plaintiff, who was the first remainderman of inheritance, and the value of the other was to be invested according to the settlement, &c.

Tenant for life entitled to dividends.

The frame of the settlement in that case was perhaps the reason of the latter part of the order being so drawn as to give the tenant for life an interest, but this course afterwards became general. Thus in *Delapole* v. *Delapole*,[3] upon the bill of an infant tenant in tail against his father the tenant for life; an inquiry was directed what timber was proper to be felled, and whether it would be for the benefit of all parties that it should be felled and sold, and the money laid out in other estates to be settled to the same uses. This case was the stronger as the will by which the property was settled contained a proviso that

[3] 17 Ves. 150; see also *Mildmay* v. *Mildmay*, 4 Bro. C. C. 76; *Wickham* v. *Wickham*, 19 Ves. 419.

in case any person becoming entitled in possession should cut down any trees his estate should cease.

Latterly the practice seems to have followed the case of *Tooker* v. *Annesley*,[4] where an inquiry was directed whether there were any and what timber trees standing in the woods and plantations on the testator's estate, which were in a state of decay, and which would not improve by standing, or the standing of which would be prejudicial to the other trees, and which it would be for the benefit of all parties interested in the estate to have felled and sold; and the Master having reported upon this inquiry, it was ordered upon further directions, that the trees mentioned in the Master's report should be felled and sold, and the proceeds brought into court and invested, and that the dividends should be paid to the tenant for life.

A dowress.

In like manner a dowress would receive one third of the income.[5]

[4] 5 Sim. 237; *Consett* v. *Bell*, 1 Y. & C. C. C. 573; *Tollemache* v. *Tollemache*, 1 Hare. 456; *Ferrand* v. *Wilson*, 4 Hare, 381; *Gent* v. *Harrison*, J. 523; Seton on Decrees.

[5] *Dickin* v. *Hamer*, 1 Dr. & Sm. 284; *Bishop* v. *Bishop*, 5 Jur. 931; 10 L. J. Ch. (N. S.) 302.

CHAP. I.
Sect. 4.
Application of corpus of fund.

If the estate of a tenant for life without impeachment of waste comes into possession before any remainder of inheritance, he is entitled to receive the corpus of the fund produced by timber rightfully cut.[6]

Leases and Sales of Settled Estates Act.

An application to the Court for the sale of timber (not ornamental) may now be made under the Leases and Sales of Settled Estates Acts.[7] The manner of dealing with the purchase-money prescribed in sect. 23 does not seem to be entirely in accordance with the rules previously existing.

Timber on glebe.

It is said that the Court of Chancery would have no difficulty on a proper application in directing timber on glebe land to be cut and the produce to be applied for the benefit of the living.[8]

Application of fund produced by ornamental

When a fund is formed by a tenant for life without impeachment of waste committing equi-

[6] *Waldo* v. *Waldo*, 12 Sim. 107; *Phillips* v. *Barlow*, 14 Sim. 263. Timber money has been said to be of the nature of real estate until something is done to convert it, *Field* v. *Brown*, 27 Beav. 90; see *Tullitt* v. *Tullitt*, Amb. 370 and post. As to timber wrongfully cut, see *Gent* v. *Harrison*, J. 517.

[7] 19 & 20 Vict. c. 120, s. 11.

[8] *Duke of Marlborough* v. *St. John*, 5 De G. & S. 179.

CHAP. I. Sect. 4.

table waste, as by wrongfully cutting ornamental timber, it is quite clear that he will not be allowed to take any interest in it.[9] Some of the authorities treat it as belonging to the first owner of the inheritance, and others as following the uses of the settlement.

timber wrongfully cut.

Rolt v. Somerville.

In *Rolt* v. *Somerville*,[1] the defendant's wife was tenant for life, remainder to the plaintiff for life, both without impeachment of waste, with remainders over. The defendant cut ornamental timber and committed other equitable waste. The bill was brought to compel the defendant to account for the money raised by these particulars and to put the estate in the same plight and condition as before. The defendant demurred: Lord Hardwicke said, " My only doubt is as to the trees that have been cut down, for if this bill had been brought before such trees had been cut down as were for the ornament or shelter of the estate this Court would have interposed; but here the mischief is done, and it is impossible to restore it to the same condition as to the plantations, and,

[9] *Wellesley* v. *Wellesley*, 6 Sim. 497; *Lushington* v. *Boldero*, 15 Beav. 1.

[1] 2 Eq. Ab. 759.

CHAP. I.
Sect. 4.

therefore, it can lie in satisfaction only; and I cannot say the plaintiff is entitled to a satisfaction for the timber which is a damage to the inheritance." And the demurrer was allowed as to this part of the bill. It is not stated whether the inheritance was represented in this suit.

Butler v. *Kynersley.*

This case was followed in *Butler* v. *Kynersley.*[2] There Kynersley was tenant for life without impeachment of waste, remainder to his sons in tail, remainder (subject to the life interest of Clarke in a moiety) to the Marchioness of Ormonde (Clarke's daughter) for life without impeachment of waste, remainder to her children in tail, with remainder (subject to a term of 1000 years for raising money) to Clarke in fee. There were never any sons of Kynersley or children of the Marchioness of Ormonde.

In 1805 and 1806 Kynersley felled ornamental timber.

In 1807, Clarke and the Marquis and Marchioness of Ormonde obtained an injunction to stay such waste.

[2] 5 Mad. 369, nom. *Ormonde* v. *Kynersley* (see *Morse* v. *Ormonde*, 5 Mad. 99). In House of Lords, 2 Bli. N. S. 374, on reference back, 7 L. J. Ch. 150; 8 L. J. Ch. 67 (decided 1830).

In 1809, Clarke by deed conveyed all his interest in the estate to the Marquis of Ormonde and his heirs.

In 1815 Kynersley died.

In 1816 the Marquis and Marchioness of Ormonde filed a bill against the personal representative of Kynersley, praying that an account might be taken of the produce of the said ornamental timber, and that the defendant might be compelled to pay the same to the plaintiffs or into court, for the benefit of the person or persons ultimately to be entitled to the inheritance of the estates.

It was urged for the plaintiffs that "In equitable waste the legal title to the timber was in the tenant for life; if, therefore, the analogy of law were to be followed, the timber felled would belong to him. But a Court of equity attached a trust upon him;[3] and for whom was this trust to be created? for all persons who might be successively interested under the limitations to which the estate was subject." Nevertheless the bill

[3] See 5 Mad. 369; *Kingham* v. *Lee*, 15 Sim. 399; *Powys* v. *Blagrave*, Kay, 501; 4 D. M. G. 448; *Micklethwaite* v. *Micklethwaite*, 1 D. & J. 504.

CHAP. I. Sect. 4.

was dismissed on the ground that the property in the timber belonged to Clarke, who at the time of the cutting had a vested inheritance in fee, and that the conveyance of this estate by the deed of 1809 did not pass any interest in waste already committed.

It is curious that three cases have since occurred in which neither *Rolt* v. *Somerville* nor *Butler* v. *Kynersley* was cited, and in which it has been decided or assumed that the proceeds of ornamental timber wrongfully cut follow the uses of the settlement.[4]

The principle of *Butler* v. *Kynersley* seems to be that as regards ornamental timber the tenant for life is to be deemed impeachable of waste, and that the property is to go as the law under such circumstances would carry it. It is not easy to see what would be the result of this doctrine in a case like *Turner* v. *Wright*,[5] where the wrongdoer had the fee subject to an executory devise over.

[4] *Wellesley* v. *Wellesley*, 6 Sim. 503 (1834); *Duke of Leeds* v. *Earl Amherst*, 16 Sim. 431; 2 Phil. 125 (1846); *Lushington* v. *Boldero*, 13 Beav. 418; 15 Beav. 1 (1851); see note, 15 Beav. 9.

[5] J. 740; 2 D. F. & J. 234. See *Blake* v. *Peters*, Addenda.

Sect. 4.

Ornamental timber rightfully cut.

Ornamental timber may also be cut rightfully. It was said in *Butler* v. *Kynersley*,[6] *arguendo*, that "There were cases in which the Court had directed timber which was in the nature of ornamental timber to be felled; and in those instances it had directed the produce of the sale to be subject to the same limitations as the estate." The principle upon which ornamental timber may be thinned is laid down in *Lushington* v. *Boldero*,[7] where an inquiry was directed—whether timber cut by the defendants had been planted or left standing for ornament or shelter, and whether any and which of the timber and other trees so cut and sold, injured or impeded the growth of any other trees adjoining thereto, which were of so much importance to the purposes of ornament and shelter intended by the devisor, that the removal of the timber or other trees so cut or sold was essential to such purposes of ornament or shelter. It was said that the fact of trees being decayed or injuring the adjoining timber did not by itself justify their removal, because trees most essential for ornament or shelter, and best entitled

[6] 7 L. J. Ch. 150; 8 L. J. Ch. 67.

[7] G. Coop. 216; 6 Mad. 149. Seton on Decrees, 3rd ed. 891.

CHAP. I.
Sect. 4.

to the protection of the Court, might be decayed and might injure the trees adjoining.

Property in ornamental timber rightfully cut.

As the equitable restraint upon a tenant for life without impeachment of waste is only to prevent him from making an unconscientious use of his legal power, there seems to be ground for contending that the property in all timber rightfully cut, whether ornamental or not, vests in him in equity as well as at law.

Timber cut on the estate of an infant.

Where there is an infant tenant in tail in possession, the Court will authorise the cutting of all timber which is fit and proper to be cut in a due course of management,[8] and the produce will be considered as personal estate.[9] But where the infant has the fee the produce seems to be real estate.[1]

Timber cut on the estate of a lunatic.

The committees of a lunatic may cut timber for repairs as a prudent owner would do,[2] and where decaying timber was properly cut on the estate[3]

[8] *Saville* v. *Saville*, Ca. temp. Talb. 16; 1 Ves. S. 548; Amb. 371; *Lyddal* v. *Clavering*, Amb. 371 (see *Rook* v. *Warth*, 1 Ves. S. 461); *Hussey* v. *Hussey*, 5 Mad. 44; *Ferrand* v. *Wilson*, 4 Hare, 382.

[9] *Tullitt* v. *Tullitt*, Amb. 370; 1 Dick. 322.

[1] *Mason* v. *Mason*, Amb. 371; 1 West. 449. See *Field* v. *Brown*, 27 Beav. 90.

[2] *Ex parte Ludlow*, 2 Atk. 407.

[3] Apparently held in fee simple.

of a lunatic, the produce of the sale was dealt with as personal assets.[4]

Practice.

If a tenant for life is restrained from felling timber by an interlocutory injunction which is not ultimately sustained, in the event of his dying before the injunction is taken off, he will lose the value of the trees which he would otherwise have cut. The plaintiff, therefore, in such a case is required to give security to the tenant for life for the value of all the trees which he may be so prevented from cutting.[5]

It appears that if a tenant for life liable to waste sells timber, he cannot prevent the vendee from cutting it.[6]

Two early cases.

In two early cases remaindermen whose estates gave them a right of waste were allowed to cut timber before coming into possession, the circumstances being such as would probably not be held now to entitle them to that privilege. In the first,[7] a term was demised to trustees for

[4] *Ex parte Bromfield*, 1 Ves. J. 453; *Oxenden* v. *Lord Compton*, 2 Ves. J. 69, 261. See *Marquis of Annandale* v. *Marchioness of Annandale*, 2 Ves. S. 383.

[5] *Wombwell* v. *Bellasyse*, 6 Ves. 110 d; *Marker* v. *Marker*, 9 Hare, 22.

[6] *Wentworth* v. *Turner*, 3 Ves. 3.

[7] *Aspinwall* v. *Leigh*, 2 Vern. 218; 1 Eq. Ab. 400.

CHAP. I. Sect. 4.

the payment of debts, and by will of the same date the reversion was devised to the plaintiff for life without impeachment of waste, with remainders over. The trustees being in possession, the Court allowed the plaintiff to cut timber to the amount of 500*l.*, upon an allegation that he was in great want, and that much timber was decaying. Again,[8] one Morris Claxton devised lands to his widow for life, remainder to the plaintiff in fee upon condition that he should pay certain legacies, and upon default over. The widow refused to allow the plaintiff to cut any timber during her lifetime, in order, as the bill alleged, that he might be compelled to commit a forfeiture by non-payment of the legacies. The Court allowed the plaintiff to take sufficient timber for payment of the legacies, making compensation to the widow for breaking the ground, &c.

Timber estate.

It must be borne in mind that general propositions respecting waste in trees are subject to exceptions when applied to what are called timber estates, where for many purposes severed

[8] *Claxton* v. *Claxton*, 2 Vern. 152.

timber is to be treated as annual rents and profits.[9]

Sect. 5.—WASTE IN MINERALS, &c.

Sect. 5.

Ownership of several minerals.

The ownership of severed minerals vests in a similar manner to that of severed trees,[1] and by custom a copyholder may have a right to take any material, such as limestone, marl, clay, or gravel, as well as trees for repairs, or the necessary purposes of his occupation,[2] and it is possible that such a privilege exists without reference to custom.[3] By custom, also, the proprietary right in minerals, &c., may be attached to a copyhold of inheritance, or for life, with power to renew or nominate a successor, so that a copyholder may sell them off the manor.[4]

If there be a grant of lands,[5] or of lands and

[9] *Ferrand* v. *Wilson*, 4 Hare, 373; *Briggs* v. *Lord Oxford*, 1 D. M. & G. 363; *Bridges* v. *Stephens*, 2 Swanst. 150, *n.* ante, p. 8; *Lord Lovat* v. *Duchess of Leeds*, 10 W. R. 398.

[1] Bainbridge on Mines, 17; *Parrott* v. *Palmer*, 3 My. & K. 636; *Gresley* v. *Mousley*, 10 W. R. 225.

[2] Bainbridge on Mines, 22; Gilb. Ten. 327; Scriven, Copyholds, 4th edit. 619.

[3] *Heydon* v. *Smith*, 13 Rep. 68.

[4] Scriven, 4th edit. p. 427; *Bishop of Winchester* v. *Knight*, 1 P. W. 406; *Marquis of Salisbury* v. *Gladstone*, 10 W. R. 930.

[5] *Saunders' Case*, 5 Rep. 12 a.

Chap. I. Sect. 5. Right of tenant for life or years.

mines expressly,[6] a tenant for life or years may work mines already open, but may not open new ones. Lord Coke says, that if there be no open mines, and a lease is made of the land, together with all mines thereon, then the lessee may dig for mines therein, otherwise the grant would be void; but the dictum is of doubtful authority.

Turbary.

Some Irish cases show that a demise of land and bog does not authorise a tenant in cutting turf for sale, unless it has always been so cut; but if the demise be of the bog alone, the rule may be different.[7]

Estovers.

If there are open limestone quarries on the land demised, it is said that the tenant may work them for estovers, but not for sale, the analogy to open mines not holding in such a case.[8] There

[6] Co. Litt. 54 b; *Astry* v. *Ballard*, 2 Lev. 185 (in a MS. note to the copy of Levinz, in Lincoln's Inn Library, it is said that the word "mines" did not occur); S. C., 2 T. Jon. 71; 3 Keb. 709, 723, 761, 765; 2 Mod. 193; *Lord Darcy* v. *Askwith*, Hob. 234; *Whitfield* v. *Bewit*, 2 P. W. 242; Scriven, Copyholds, 4th edit. p. 427, notes.

[7] *Chatterton* v. *White*, 1 Ir. Eq. 200; *White* v. *Walsh*, Jon. (Ir.) 626; *Lord Waterpark* v. *Austen*, Jon. (Ir.) 627; *Coppinger* v. *Gubbins*, 3 J. & L. 397; *Moore* v. *Orr*, 8 Ir. C. L. 347; *Hargrove* v. *Lord Congleton*, 12 Ir. C. L. 362, 368.

[8] *Mansfield* v. *Crawford*, 9 Ir. Eq. 271; *Purcell* v. *Nash*, Jon. (Ir.) 625.

may also be estovers of other constituent parts of the inheritance, as turf,[9] gravel and clay,[1] and coal.[2]

Tenant for life impeachable of waste.

A tenant for life impeachable of waste has a right to continue the working of mines, claypits, &c., where the settlor, or a preceding tenant in tail, has done it, and he may sink new shafts for the purpose of following up a vein of coal; but it is very doubtful whether such a tenant for life has a right to open pits or mines which have been abandoned, or the preparations for opening which have not been completed. And there seems to be no authority on the question whether a new vein or bed may be worked by means of an old shaft.[3]

Tenant for life without impeachment of waste.

A tenant for life without impeachment of waste has of course a right to open new mines.[4]

Dowress.

The rights of a dowress in mines opened after her husband's death have been discussed, but not decided.[5]

[9] *De Salis* v. *Crossan*, 1 Ball & Beat. 188; *Lord Courton* v. *Ward*, 1 Sch. & Lef. 8; *De Salis* v. ——, 2 Moll. 516; *Howley* v. *Jebb*, 8 Ir. C. L. 435.

[1] Co. Litt. 53 b.

[2] 2 Rol. Abr. 816.

[3] *Clavering* v. *Clavering*, 2 P. W. 388; *Viner* v. *Vaughan*, 2 Beav. 467.

[4] *Countess of Plymouth* v. *Lady Archer*, 1 Bro. C. C. 159.

[5] *Dickin* v. *Hamer*, 1 Dr. & Sm. 284.

Chap. 1.

Sect. 5.
Practice.

A court of equity will not try the right to the possession of a mine because an account of the mesne profits will have to be taken.[6]

Delay.

It is a clear rule that parties seeking relief in mining cases are bound to be very prompt in making their application;[7] and in *Parrott* v. *Palmer*,[8] which was a bill filed by the lord of a manor against certain tenants and their under-lessees, the laches of the plaintiff, which was considerable, was held to have disentitled him to an account, as well as to an injunction.

Sect. 6.

Sect. 6.—WASTE IN BUILDINGS.[9]

Loss by fire.

At the common law, where a house was burned down by negligence or mischance, it was waste; but as to such fires the landlord's action against

[6] *Vice* v. *Thomas*, 4 Y. & C. 538; *Sayer* v. *Pierce*, 1 Ves. S. 232.

[7] *Clavering* v. *Clavering*, 2 P. W. 388; *Norway* v. *Rowe*, 19 Ves. 143; *Field* v. *Beaumont*, 1 Swanst. 208; *Clegg* v. *Edmondson*, 3 Jur. N. S. 299.

[8] 3 My. & K. 636.

[9] See also next section.

the tenant has been taken away by statute.[1] A lessee who covenants generally to repair, is still bound to rebuild after a fire;[2] and whether the lessee is bound to rebuild or not, he remains liable to pay the rent.[3]

A devisee for life, with a condition against committing any manner of waste, and for keeping the premises in good and tenantable repair, became lunatic, and they were subsequently destroyed by accidental fire. In order to prevent the risk of forfeiture it was held that the premises ought to be rebuilt at the expense of the lunatic's estate.[4]

Permissive waste.

When a tenant for life suffers buildings to go to decay, that is permissive waste, and courts of equity do not in general interfere with it,[5] but

[1] Co. Litt. 53*b*; 6 Anne, c. 31; 14 Geo. 3, c. 78; and see *Re Skingley*, 3 Mac. & Gor. 221; *Rook* v. *Warth*, 1 Ves. S. 460; *White* v. *M'Cann*, 1 Ir. C. L. 205; Gale on Easements, 3rd edit. p. 339.

[2] *Bullock* v. *Dommitt*, 6 T. R. 650.

[3] *Holtzapfell* v. *Baker*, 18 Ves. 115; *Leeds* v. *Cheetham*, 1 Sim. 146; *Lofts* v. *Dennis*, 7 W. R. 199.

[4] *Re Skingley*, 3 Mac. & Gor. 221; *Powys* v. *Blagrave*, Kay, 502; 4 D. M. & G. 448; *Gregg* v. *Coates*, 23 Beav. 33.

[5] *Powys* v. *Blagrave*, Kay, 495; 4 D. M. & G. 448; *Castlemaine* v. *Craven*, 2 Eq. Ab. 758; 22 Vin. 523; *Turner* v. *Busk*, 22 Vin. 523; *Wood* v. *Gaynon*, 1 Amb. 395; *Lansdowne*

they may do so under special circumstances. Thus, in *Caldwall* v. *Baylis*,[6] copyholds were devised to A. for life, and after his decease to B. in fee; but if he should die in the lifetime of A., then to the plaintiffs as tenants in common. A. permitted the premises to go to decay during the life of B., who had intended to commence proceedings against him in consequence of his neglect, but desisted upon his promise to repair forthwith. B. died, and A. having neglected to perform his promise either during B.'s lifetime, or since his death, the buildings grew ruinous for want of the needful repairs. An injunction was granted to restrain A. from permitting or suffering any further waste.[7] In *Marsh* v. *Wells*,[8] a person entitled to leasehold property subject to a

v. *Lansdowne*, 1 Mad. 116; 1 J. & W. 522; *Warren* v. *Rudall*, *Ex parte Godfrey*, 29 L. J. Ch. 543, 1 J. & H. 1. As to action at law, see Sect. 4. Lord Hardwicke is reported to have charged a tenant for life without impeachment of waste, with sums for the repairs of tenants' houses. *Parteriche* v. *Powlet*, 2 Atk. 383; *Blake* v. *Peters*, V.-C. K. See Addenda.

[6] 2 Mer. 408.

[7] Permissive waste is a cause of forfeiture of copyholds; but equity will in general relieve against it. Scriven on Copyholds, 4th edit. pp. 442, 463; *Andrews* v. *Hulse*, 4 K. & J. 392.

[8] 2 S. & S. 87; *Powys* v. *Blagrave*, Kay, 503; 4 D. M. & G. 448.

previous life interest therein, renewed the lease with the consent of the tenant for life, and covenanted to repair, the tenant for life having neglected to keep the premises in repair, his estate was held liable to indemnify the covenantor.

Equitable waste in houses.

The legal powers of a tenant for life without impeachment of waste to deal with the buildings as he pleases, are very much limited by the doctrine of equitable waste. In the *Raby Castle Case*,[9] which, although not the earliest, is the leading authority on this subject, the tenant for life was pulling down the principal mansion-house, and he was decreed to repair and rebuild it, and put it in the same plight and condition it was in at the time of his entry thereon. The decree not having been performed in Lord Barnard's lifetime, an issue was directed to charge his assets with the value of the damages.[1]

Rolt v. *Somerville.*

In *Rolt* v. *Somerville*,[2] several houses, out-buildings, and lead water-pipes were ordered to

[9] *Vane* v. *Barnard*, Prec. Ch. 454 ; 2 Vern. 738 ; Gilb. Eq. Rep. 127 ; 1 Eq. Ab. 399 ; 1 Salkeld, 161.

[1] 2 Eq. Ab. 759 ; *Duke of Leeds* v. *Earl Amherst*, 14 Sim. 357 ; 2 Phil. 117.

[2] 2 Eq. Ab. 759.

CHAP. I.
Sect. 6.

be restored; and in *Aston* v. *Aston*,[3] Lord Hardwicke said, "If tenant for life without impeachment of waste pulled down farmhouses, in general I should no more scruple restraining him than I should from pulling down the mansion-house (unless where he pulled down two to make into one, in order to bear the burthen but of one), it tending equally to the destruction of the thing settled."

Micklethwaite v. *Micklethwaite.*

In *Micklethwaite* v. *Micklethwaite*,[4] the defendant was tenant for life, "without impeachment of or for any manner of waste, other than and except voluntary waste in pulling down houses or buildings, and not rebuilding the same, or others of equal or greater value." He sold the mansion-house for old materials, and commenced pulling it down with the view of building a new one. The bill asked, amongst other things, that the defendant might be decreed to complete a suitable mansion,[5] and to give sufficient security, to be approved of by the Court, for its completion; and that an account might be taken of

[3] 1 Ves. S. 265; *Blake* v. *Peters*, V.-C. K. See Addenda.
[4] 1 D. & J. 504.
[5] 1 D. & J. 504.

the proceeds of the sale of the materials of the mansion-house, and that such proceeds might be invested. The defendant had commenced preparations for building the new house, and upon his undertaking to continue them with reasonable despatch, the cause was ordered to stand over generally, with liberty to apply.

Where[6] a tenant for life, without impeachment of waste, pulled down the mansion-house, and rebuilt it on another part of the property, using the old materials for that purpose, he was not charged with equitable waste, but it was suggested that he might have been so charged if the old. materials had been sold. The estate had been improved by the building of the new mansion, and the pulling down of the old one, but the Court did not proceed upon that.[7]

[6] *Morris* v. *Morris*, 6 W. R. 427 ; 7 W. R. 249 ; 3 D. & J. 323.

[7] See 2 Will. Saunders, p. 259 ; Eden on Injunctions, p. 150 ; ante, Sect. 1, Meliorating Waste ; *Smyth* v. *Carter*, 18 Beav. 78.

CHAP. I.
Sect. 7.

Sect. 7.—LANDLORD AND TENANT.[8]

The relation of a tenant to his landlord as respects the treatment of the premises demised, is usually defined by the custom of the country, or by express agreement, the tenant remaining in addition under the obligations imposed by the common law, except so far as they may be excluded by the terms of the tenancy.[9] Thus, an action for waste lies against a tenant for years, although his lease contains a covenant relating to the same subject,[1] also against a tenant holding over after the determination of his lease,[2] or the expiration of a notice to quit.[3]

Permissive waste.

An action on the case for permissive waste will not lie against a tenant at will,[4] nor against a tenant from year to year, their obligation, in the absence of special agreement, only being to use

[8] See also Sect. 6.

[9] *Phillips* v. *Smith*, 14 M. & W. 589.

[1] *Kenlyside* v. *Thornton*, 2 W. Bla. 1111; *Marker* v. *Kenrick*, 17 Jur. 44.

[2] *Torriano* v. *Young*, 6 C. & P. 8.

[3] *Burchell* v. *Hornsby*, 1 Camp. 360.

[4] Litt. s. 71; Co. Litt. 53 a; 5 Rep. 13 b; Cro. Eliz. 777, 784; *Panton* v. *Isham*, 3 Lev. 359; 1 Salk. 19; *Gibson* v. *Wells*, 1 B. & P. N. R. 290.

the premises in a husbandlike manner.[5] Whether such an action lies against tenants for years or for life is also doubtful.[6]

Breaches of covenant.

Strictly speaking, acts contrary to the obligation of a tenant to deal with the premises according to the custom of the country or express agreement, are not waste unless they are also breaches of the common law, but being of a like mischief with acts of waste, they are restrained upon a like principle.[7]

Cases in which injunctions have been applied for.

Injunctions have been applied for to restrain a tenant:—

From removing dung, crops, &c., from the premises:[8]

[5] *Ferguson* v. —, 2 Esp. 590; *Horsefall* v. *Mather*, Holt, N. P. c. 7; *Powley* v. *Walker*, 5 T. R. 373; *Herne* v. *Bembow*, 4 Taunt. 764; *Auworth* v. *Johnson*, 5 C. & P. 239; *Torriano* v. *Young*, 6 C. & P. 8. See *White* v. *M'Cann*, 1 Ir. C. L. 205.

[6] Litt. s. 71; 5 Rep. 13 b.; Cro. Eliz. 777, 784; 2 Inst. 145; Co. Litt. 53 a; 2 Rol. Ab. 828; 1 Will. Saunders, 323 c; *Cudlip* v. *Rundle*, Carth. 203; *Herne* v. *Bembow*, 4 Taunt. 764; *Jones* v. *Hill*, 7 Taunt. 392; 1 Moore, 100; *Harnett* v. *Maitland*, 16 M. & W. 257; *Re Skingley*, 3 Mac. & Gor. 221. See Jarm. Conv., 3rd edit. p. 409, and *White* v. *M'Cann*, 1 Ir. C. L. 205.

[7] *Songhurst* v. *Dixey*, Toth. 255; *Kimpton* v. *Eve*, 2 Ves. & B. 352.

[8] *Johnson* v. *Goldwaine*, 3 Anst. 749; citing *Grant* v. *Lord Belfast*; *Pulteney* v. *Skelton*, 5 Ves. 147, 260; *Lathropp* v. *Marsh*, 5 Ves. 259; *Onslow* v. —, 16 Ves. 173; *Kimpton* v. *Eve*, 2 Ves. & B. 349. Query whether this doctrine applies only to outgoing tenants. Eden on Injunctions, 198.

From sowing the land with pernicious seeds:[9]

From breaking up ancient meadow or pasture,[1] a bowling green,[2] or rabbit warren:[3]

From removing buildings and landlord's fixtures:[4]

From converting the premises to a different use,[5] as to the purposes of a school:[6]

[9] *Pratt* v. *Brett*, 2 Mad. 62.

[1] Co. Litt., 53 b.; Toth. 114, 209, 210; Ch. Rep. 13; Fin. 189; *Johnson* v. *Goldwaine*, 3 Anst. 749; *Woodward* v. *Gyles*, 2 Vern. 119; *Rolfe* v. *Peterson*, 2 Bro. P. C. 2nd edit. p. 436; *Worsley* v. *Stuart*, 4 Bro. P. C., 2nd edit. p. 377; *Simmons* v. *Morton*, 7 Bing. 640; *Lathropp* v. *Marsh*, 5 Ves. 259; *Pulteney* v. *Skelton*, 5 Ves. 260; *Lord Grey de Wilton* v. *Saxon*, 6 Ves. 106; *Drury* v. *Molins*, 6 Ves. 328; *Goring* v. *Goring*, 3 Swanst. 661; *Duke of St. Albans* v. *Skipwith*, 8 Beav. 354; *Martin* v. *Coggan*, 1 Hog. 120; *Joley* v. *Stockley*, 1 Hog. 247; *Morris* v. *Morris*, 1 Hog. 238; *Shew* v. *Weir*, 1 Ir. Eq. 213; *Creag* v. *Carmichael*, 7 Ir. Eq. 334; *French* v. *Macale*, 2 Dr. & W. 269.

[2] *City of London* v. *Pugh*, 4 Bro. P. C. 395.

[3] *Angerstein* v. *Hunt*, 6 Ves. 488; not waste at common law, see *Lurting* v. *Conn*, 1 Ir. Ch. 273.

[4] *Geast* v. *Lord Belfast*, 3 Anst. 749; *Mayor of London* v. *Hedger*, 18 Ves. 355; *Kimpton* v. *Eve*, 2 Ves. & B. 349; *Sheriff* v. *Barnard*, 8 Sim. 165; *Pratt* v. *Brett*, 2 Mad. 62; *Smyth* v. *Carter*, 18 Beav. 78; *Duke of Beaufort* v. *Bates*, 10 W. R. 149, 200.

[5] *Brydges* v. *Kilburne*, 5 Ves. 689, 691; *Bennett* v. *Sadler*, 14 Ves. 526; *Worden* v. *Ellers*, cited Eden on Injunctions, p. 199; *Hunt* v. *Browne*, Sausse & Scully, 178.

[6] *Kemp* v. *Sober*, 1 Sim. N. S. 517; on appeal, 19 L. T. 308; *Johnstone* v. *Hall*, 2 K. & J. 414.

From destroying timber or other trees, underwood, or fences:[7]

From turning goats into a young wood:[8]

From allowing the banks of a river[9] or fish-pond[1] to get out of repair:

From removing mineral substances deposited by a stream.[2]

In *Ward* v. *Duke of Buckingham*[3] in the House of Lords, upon a lease of alum works, with a covenant by the lessee to leave stock of a certain amount upon the premises, there being a fair ground of suspicion that he did not intend to perform his covenant in that respect, a decree in the nature of a decree *quia timet* was made to prevent a breach.

Distinction between waste and breaches of agreement.

Some of the foregoing are cases of waste at the common law, and others of breaches of agreement. This distinction has been drawn; that whereas acts of pure waste are restrained on

7 *Pratt* v. *Brett*, 2 Mad. 62; *Lambert* v. *Lambert*, 2 Ir. Eq. 210; *Doran* v. *Carroll*, 11 Ir. Ch. 379.

8 *Rogers* v. *Price*, 13 Jur. 821; see *Doe* d. *Rogers* v. *Price*, 19 L. J. C. P. 121.

9 *Lord Kilmorey* v. *Thackeray*, 2 Bro. C. C. 65.

1 *Earl Bathurst* v. *Burden*, 2 Bro. C. C. 69.

2 *Thomas* v. *Jones*, 1 Y. & C. C. C. 526.

3 Cited by Lord Eldon, 10 Ves. 161.

Chap. I. Sect. 7.

the ground of irreparable damage, in cases of contract the person entitled in possession subject to the lease has a right to insist on the performance of the stipulations, *modo et formâ*, irrespective of the question of damage.[4] This privilege, however, appears in some cases to be confined to the immediate reversioner. Thus, where[5] a lessee for 999 years covenanted not to use the premises as a school, and the reversion was afterwards devised to A. for life, with remainder to his children in tail, with remainder to B. for life, with remainder to her first son in tail, with remainders over, and the lessee broke the covenant in collusion with A. who was a bachelor, it was held that B. and her son could not have an injunction before they became entitled to the receipt of the rents.

Altered state of the property.

Where the agreement broken was entered into with reference to a state of the property which has ceased to exist through no fault of the tenant, the landlord will be left to his remedy at law.[6]

[4] *Kemp* v. *Sober*, 1 Sim. N. S. 520; on appeal, 19 L. T. 308. This doctrine perhaps only applies to stipulations giving rights clearly in excess of the Common Law rights of the parties. See *Lambert* v. *Lambert*, 2 Ir. Eq. 210; *Doran* v. *Carroll*, 11 Ir. Ch. 379; and see 3 D. M. G. 321.

[5] *Johnstone* v. *Hall*, 2 K. & J. 414; see *Tipping* v. *Eckersley*, 2 K. & J. 264.

[6] *Duke of Bedford* v. *Trustees of the British Museum*, 2 My.

Underlessee.

An injunction will be granted to a ground landlord to stay waste in an underlessee.[7]

Liquidated damages.

If the lessee is at liberty to plough meadow land, or otherwise convert the premises upon paying an additional rent, of course he will not be restrained from doing so.[8]

Landlord restrained.

In connection with this subject it may be noticed, that where a lease was made reserving the trees, an injunction was granted to restrain the landlord from cutting ornamental trees on a lawn, the tenant having laid out money in a plan of improvement to which the landlord had consented, and of which these trees formed part.[9]

& K. 552; *Roper* v. *Williams*, T. & R. 18; *Wood* v. *Sutcliffe*, 2 Sim. N. S. 163.

[7] *Farrant* v. *Lovell*, 3 Atk. 723; see *Lord Norbury* v. *Alleyne*, 1 Dr. & Walsh, 337; *Keogh* v. *Collins*, Hay & J. 805.

[8] *Aylett* v. *Dodd*, 2 Atk. 239; *Woodward* v. *Gyles*, 2 Vern. 119; *Ponsonby* v. *Adams*, 2 Bro. P. C. 2nd edit. 431; *Rolfe* v. *Peterson*, 2 Bro. P. C. 2nd edit. 436; *Hardy* v. *Martin*, 1 Cox, 26; *Forbes* v. *Carney*, Wallis, 38; *Jones* v. *Green*, 3 Y. & J. 298; *Molony* v. *Quail*, 4 Law Rec. N. S. 107; *Maxwell* v. *Mitchell*, 1 Ir. Eq. R. 359; *Burne* v. *Madden*, Ll. & G. temp. P. 493; *Smith* v. *Ryan*, 9 Ir. L. 235; *French* v. *Macale*, 2 Dr. & Warren, 269; *City of London* v. *Pugh*, 4 Bro. P. C. 2nd edit. 395.

[9] *Jackson* v. *Cater*, 5 Ves. 688; see *Duke of Leeds* v. *Earl Amherst*, 2 Phil. 123.

Sect. 8.—MORTGAGOR AND MORTGAGEE.

Mortgagee in possession.

In general a mortgagee in possession must not commit waste,[1] and he is bound to do necessary repairs.[2] When the security is insufficient he may, however, cut timber or open and work mines at his own risk in case of loss, and applying the profits (if any) in reduction of the principal and interest due;[3] but if the security is sufficient, and he has no authority from the mortgagor,[4] he will, under similar circumstances, be charged with his receipts and disallowed his expenses.[5] If the mortgage be of an open mine, the mortgagee is entitled to work it as a prudent owner would do, and he is not bound to advance money for speculative improvements.

[1] *Farrant* v. *Lovel*, 3 Atk. 723; *Hardy* v. *Reeves*, 4 Ves. 480; *Sandon* v. *Hooper*, 6 Beav. 249; *Anon.* 1 L. J. Ch. 119.

[2] *Godfrey* v. *Watson*, 3 Atk. 518; Seton on Decrees, vol. i, p. 398.

[3] Lord St. Leonards' Handy Book, p. 92; *Witherington* v. *Banks*, Sel. Ca. Ch. 30; *Millett* v. *Davy*, M. R., 19th Nov., 1862.

[4] *Norton* v. *Cooper*, 25 L. J. Ch. 151.

[5] *Thorneycroft* v. *Crockett*, 16 Sim. 445; *Hood* v. *Easton*, 2 Giff. 692; see *Hughes* v. *Williams*, 12 Ves. 493.

[6] *Rowe* v. *Wood*, 2 J. & W. 556.

Where[7] a mortgagee in possession committed waste pending a redemption suit, he was ordered on motion to deliver up the premises to the mortgagor.

Mortgagor in possession.

If the mortgagor is in possession, and the security is insufficient, he will be restrained from cutting timber.[8] The meaning of the term 'insufficient' is thus explained[9] by Wigram, V.-C.: "I think the question which must be tried is, whether the property the mortgagee takes as a security is sufficient in this sense—that the security is worth so much more than the money advanced—that the act of cutting timber is not to be considered as substantially impairing the value, which was the basis of the contract between the parties at the time it was entered into." And a mortgagor in possession (at all events when the security is insufficient) must

[7] *Hanson* v. *Derby*, 2 Vern. 392; and see *Robinson* v. *Maguire*, 9 Ir. Eq. 268.

[8] *Robinson* v. *Litton*, 3 Atk. 210; *Lord Blaney* v. *Mahon*, 22 Vin. Ab. 521; *Usborne* v. *Usborne*, *Hopkins* v. *Monk*, *Twedale* v. *Twedale*, cited 1 Dick. 76; *Pitman* v. *Hodges*, 1 Fowl. Ex. Pr. 241; *Cox* v. *Goodfellow*, 8 Ves. 105 a; *Humphries* v. *Harrison*, 1 J. & W. 581; *Hippesley* v. *Spencer*, 5 Mad. 422; *Fairfield* v. *Weston*, 2 S. & S. 96.

[9] *King* v. *Smith*, 2 Hare, 241; see *Leake* v. *Beckett*, 1 Y. & J. 339.

CHAP. I. Sect. 8. Underwood.

only cut underwood as a crop, in the ordinary course, *i. e.*, in a husbandlike manner, at the usual seasons and of the usual growth. A mortgagor who had become bankrupt was altogether restrained from cutting underwood until assignees had been appointed.[1]

After a decree for an account under a bill of foreclosure, the mortgagor may be restrained from committing waste, although an injunction is not prayed by the bill.[2]

Sect. 9.

Sect. 9.—ECCLESIASTICAL CORPORATIONS.

Powers of alienation at the common law.

AT the common law a dean and chapter, and any other corporation aggregate, might of themselves alone have alienated their estates as fully as a person seised in fee in his natural

[1] *Hampton* v. *Hodges*, 8 Ves. 105; *Humphries* v. *Harrison*, 1 Jac. & W. 581.

[2] *Wright* v. *Atkyns*, 1 Ves. & B. 313; *Goodman* v. *Kine*, 8 Beav. 379.

capacity might have done. But bishops, deans, parsons, and other such corporations sole, if they wished to bind their successors, must have had the confirmation of others who had the power of confirming in that behalf, and then their grants were as good as the grants of corporations aggregate.[3] Grants made by bishops required confirmation by the dean and chapter; those made by deans required confirmation by the bishop and chapter; and those made by parsons, or vicars, required confirmation by the patron and ordinary.

Rights of waste by corporations sole.

It follows that at the common law a parson, with the proper consents, having unlimited power of alienation, might dispose of timber and open mines, the patron and ordinary taking care of the interests of the Church.[4] But corporations sole, acting without confirmation, seem never to have had more extensive privileges as to timber,

[3] Watson's Clergyman's Law, 4th edit. p. 424; Co. Litt. 44 a; Jarm. Conv., 3rd edit. vol. iv. p. 244; Burn's Ecclesiastical Law, 4th edit. vol. ix. pp. 298, 368; *Blewitt* v. *Tregonning*, 3 A. & E. 556.

[4] *The Duke of Marlborough* v. *St. John*, 5 De G. & Sm. 174; see *Bishop of Winchester* v. *Wolgar*, 3 Swanst. 493; *Bishop of London* v. *Webb*, 1 P. W. 527; 2 Eq. Ab. 758.

Chap. 1.
Sect. 9.

mines, &c., than an ordinary tenant for life;[5] for example, they may work mines already open, but not open new ones.[6] It seems, however, that some acts, which are waste between landlord and tenant, are not necessarily waste in a parson.[7]

Statutes.

The statute law upon this subject is somewhat intricate.

By the 35 Edw. 1, stat. 2, parsons were prohibited from felling trees in the churchyard, except for repairs of the church and chancel.[8]

Enabling statute.

By what is called the Enabling Statute,[9] 32 H. 8, c. 28, corporations sole (except parsons and vicars) were authorised to grant leases, binding on their successors, respect being had to certain qualifications therein mentioned, some of which were, (1) That the term should not exceed

[5] Co. Litt. 341 a; *Duke of Marlborough* v. *St. John*, 5 De G. & Sm. 174; *Knight* v. *Moseley*, 1 Amb. 176; *Strachey* v. *Francis*, 2 Atk. 217; *Jefferson* v. *Bishop of Durham*, 1 B. & P. 105.

[6] *Knight* v. *Moseley*, 1 Amb. 176; *Huntley* v. *Russell*, 13 Q. B. 572; 18 L. J. Q. B. 239; 13 Jur. 837.

[7] *Duke of St. Albans* v. *Skipwith*, 8 Beav. 354; *Bird* v. *Relph*, 4 B. & Ad. 826.

[8] Thompson's Entries, 240; *Knowle* v. *Harvey*, 3 Buls. 158; 1 Rol. 335; 2 Rol. Abr. 813; *Costerd's Case*, 2 Rol. 111; *Strachey* v. *Francis*, 2 Atk. 216.

[9] Co. Litt. 44 a.

twenty-one years, or three lives; (2) That the accustomed rent at least should be reserved; (3) That the lease should not be without impeachment of waste.

Restraining statutes.

It may be remarked, that in early times the legislature was constantly struggling to check the accumulation of lands in mortmain, and we therefore naturally find that the extensive powers of alienation, which the clergy possessed at the common law, were left uncontrolled. But after the change in the constitution of the Church, and the other social changes which accompanied the Reformation, the endowments required more protection; and, accordingly, first bishops,[1] and by another group of statutes,[2] deans and chapters, parsons, vicars, &c., were altogether restrained from alienating their estates, except by way of lease, and in such manner as was by the several Acts provided.

Confirmation still required.

Leases framed in accordance with the restraining statutes, did not bind the successors without confirmation, where confirmation was necessary before. The forms of such leases were, in many

[1] 1 Eliz. c. 19; see Jac. 1, c. 3.

[2] 13 Eliz. c. 10; 14 Eliz. c. 11; 18 Eliz. c. 11.

CHAP. I.
Sect. 9.

respects, similar to that prescribed by the Enabling Statute; but it was not expressly enacted that lessees under the restraining statutes, should be impeachable of waste.[3]

Leases not made in conformity with the statutes voidable.

It seems that leases not made in conformity with these statutes are voidable only, and not void.[4]

Effect of restraining statutes on rights of waste.

Whatever difficulty there may have been in preventing corporations aggregate from committing waste when their powers of alienation were unrestricted, it was soon decided that a dean and chapter are restrained by the equity of 13 Eliz. c. 10, for making leases dispunishable of waste,[5] and it is said that 1 Eliz. c. 19, concerning the leases of bishops (made with confirmation), must have the same construction.[6]

Mining lease by incumbent.

It would seem to follow that the incumbent of a living has now no power to grant a mining lease,

[3] Co. Litt. 44 b. Recent Acts relating to this subject are 5 & 6 Vict. c. 27; 5 & 6 Vict. c. 108; 21 & 22 Vict. c. 57; 24 & 25 Vict. c. 105; see *Jenkins* v. *Green*, 27 Beav. 437, 440; 28 Beav. 87.

[4] *Doe* v. *Taniere*, 12 Q. B. 998; *Pennington* v. *Cardale*, 3 H. & N. 666.

[5] *Re Dean and Chapter of Worcester*, 6 Rep. 37 a; *Herring* v. *Dean and Chapter of St. Paul's*, 3 Swanst. 492; *Wither* v. *Dean and Chapter of Winchester*, 3 Mer. 421.

[6] Watson's Clergyman's Law, 462.

even with the consent of the patron and ordinary. For such a lease could only take effect, if at all, under the 13 Eliz. c. 10, and this statute, as construed in the case of the Dean and Chapter of Worcester, does not allow of a lease being made without impeachment of waste, even if the difficulty as to the reservation of the accustomed yearly rent could be got over.[7] But the question has been treated as a doubtful one.[8]

Ecclesiastical Commissioners.

Ecclesiastical corporations aggregate or sole may, however, grant leases for long terms of years for mining and other purposes, with the sanction of the Ecclesiastical Commissioners.[9]

Timber to be used for repairs.

Timber growing on the estates of an ecclesiastical corporation is a fund for the benefit of the church. It may be felled for the repairs of the ecclesiastical buildings.[1] So also, "A rector may cut down timber for the repairs of the parsonage house or the chancel, but not for any common

[7] *Bishop of Hereford* v. *Scory*, Cro. Eliz. 874.

[8] *Countess of Rutland's Case*, 1 Lev. 107; 1 Sid. 152; *Doe* v. *Collinge*, 7 C. B. 939; *Bartlett* v. *Phillips*, 4 D. & J. 414; *Holden* v. *Weekes*, 1 J. & H. 278.

[9] 5 & 6 Vict. c. 108; 21 & 22 Vict. c. 57.

[1] *Jefferson* v. *Bishop of Durham*, 1 B. & P. 115; *Wither* v. *Dean and Chapter of Winchester*, 3 Mer. 421; *Herring* v. *Dean and Chapter of St. Paul's*, 3 Swanst. 492.

purpose; and this he may be justified in doing under the statute 35 Edw. I., stat. 2, entitled, *Ne rector prosternat arbores in cemeterio.* If it is the custom of the country, he may cut down underwood for any purpose, but if he grubs it up it is waste. He may cut down timber likewise for repairing any old pews that belong to the rectory; and he is also entitled to botes for repairing barns and outhouses belonging to the parsonage."[2]

The statute which Lord Hardwicke cites authorises timber to be cut in the churchyard for the repairs of the church and chancel only, but it may be cut on the glebe for the purposes which he mentions. The rector may also dig stones there for similar repairs.[3]

There has been some controversy whether the timber cut must be specifically applied towards the actual repairs for which it was wanted. The rule seems to be that it may be cut and sold for the purpose of buying other timber more suitable

[2] *Strachey* v. *Francis*, 2 Atk. 216; Barn. Cha. 399; *Jefferson* v. *Bishop of Durham*, 1 B. & P. 105.

[3] *Knight* v. *Moseley*, 1 Amb. 176. The answer averred that the quarries were opened before.

for the repairs intended, but not to defray the general expenses of repairs.[4]

Remedies for waste.

Sequestration.

An incumbent is bound to put the buildings, hedges, fences, &c., in a good state of repair, and to keep them so, and the obligation will (if necessary) be enforced by sequestration of the revenues of the benefice. The incumbent for the time being may sue a predecessor or his representatives in respect of the dilapidations which he may have left, either in the Ecclesiastical Courts, or (except in the case of a bishopric) at Common Law.[5] It is well settled that the successor cannot recover damages for mismanagement of the glebe land,[6] but there is some authority that he may do so for things severed, as timber or

Successor may sue in ecclesiastical or commou law courts.

[4] *Knight* v. *Moseley*, 1 Amb. 176; *Wither* v. *Dean and Chapter of Winchester*, 3 Mer. 421; *Attorney-General* v. *Geary*, 3 Mer. 513; *Herring* v. *Dean and Chapter of St. Paul's*, 3 Swanst. 492; *Duke of Marlborough* v. *St. John*, 5 De G. & Sm. 178; see ante, Sect. 4, Estovers.

[5] Gibbon's Law of Dilapidations and Nuisances; *Wise* v. *Metcalfe*, 10 B. & C. 299; *Bird* v. *Relph*, 4 B. & Ad. 826; 2 A. & E. 773; *Bunbury* v. *Hewson*, 3 Exch. 558; *Warren* v. *Lugger*, 3 Exch. 579; *Mason* v. *Lambert*, 12 Q. B. 795; *Huntley* v. *Russell*, 13 Q. B. 572; 13 Jur. 837; 18 L. J. Q. B. 239; *Bryan* v. *Clay*, 1 E. & B. 38; *Jenkin* v. *Betham*, 16 C. B. 437; *Martin* v. *Roe*, 7 E. & B. 237; *Gleaves* v. *Parfitt*, 7 C. B. N. S. 838.

[6] *Bird* v. *Relph*, 4 B. & Ad. 826; 2 A. & E. 773; *Duke*

CHAP. 1. Sect. 9.

gravel.[7] In the administration of the predecessor's estate, this claim is postponed to that of simple contract creditors at law, but apparently not in equity.[8]

Writ of prohibition.

Lord Coke frequently asserted that a writ of prohibition[9] lay at common law against a bishop or parson committing waste, and on one occasion he is reported to have said, "and so it shall be in the case of a dean and chapter." Other preventive remedies, however, if any such ever existed, have in practice been replaced by injunctions.

Injunctions.

The right to an injunction to restrain bishops resides in the Attorney-General on behalf of the Crown, their patron, and possibly, to some extent, in the Metropolitan.[1] So a dean and

St. Albans v. *Skipwith*, 8 Beav. 354 ; see *Hoskins* v. *Fetherstone*, 2 Bro. C. C. 52.

[7] *Bird* v. *Relph*, 4 B. & Ad. 826 ; 2 A. & E. 773 ; *Huntley* v. *Russell*, 13 Q. B. 572 ; 13 Jur. 837 ; 18 L. J. Q. B. 239 ; see post, p. 79, *Bartlett* v. *Phillips*, 4 D. & J. 414; *Holden* v. *Weekes*, 1 J. & H. 278 ; *Knight* v. *Moseley*, 1 Amb. 176.

[8] *Bissett* v. *Burgess*, 23 Beav. 278.

[9] *Stockman* v. *Wither*, 1 Rol. 86 ; *Bishop of Salisbury's Case*, Godb. 259 ; see also 2 Buls. 279 ; *Costerd's Case*, 2 Rol. 111; *Drury* v. *Kent*, Hob. 36 ; 2 Rol. Abr. 813 ; *King* v. *Sakars*, 3 Bul. 91 ; Moore, 917 ; *Acland* v. *Atwell*, 3 Swanst. 499 ; *Jefferson* v. *Bishop of Durham*, 1 B. & P. 105.

[1] *Knight* v. *Moseley*, 1 Amb. 176 ; *Jefferson* v. *Bishop of

chapter may be restrained at the suit of the Crown, but not at that of a stranger.[2] In the case of a parson or vicar, the application should be made by the patron,[3] or, if he is a consenting party to the waste, by the ordinary.[4]

Ploughing glebe meadow.

We have seen that no action lies for ploughing glebe meadow,[5] and as a general rule, the Court of Chancery will not interfere to stay it:[6] but the widow of a rector who was committing this and other acts of waste during a vacancy was restrained at the suit of the patroness.[7]

Widow of rector.

Application of produce of waste.

In *Bartlett* v. *Phillips*[8] (a special case), the Court was of opinion that the produce of past waste should be laid out for the permanent improvement of the vicarage. Subsequently, in

Durham, 1 B. & P. 116, 131; *Wither* v. *Dean and Chapter of Winchester*, 3 Mer. 421.

[2] *Wither* v. *Dean and Chapter of Winchester*, 3 Mer. 421; *Herring* v. *Dean and Chapter of St. Paul's*, 3 Swanst. 492; Eden on Injunctions, p. 204; see *Acland* v. *Atwell*, 3 Swanst. 499.

[3] *Strachey* v. *Francis*, 2 Atk. 216; 1 Barn. Cha. 399; *Hoskins* v. *Fetherstone*, 2 Bro. C. C. 552; *Knight* v. *Moseley*, 1 Amb. 176; *Duke of St. Albans* v. *Skipwith*, 8 Beav. 354; *Duke of Marlborough* v. *St. John*, 5 De G. & Sm. 174.

[4] *Holden* v. *Weekes*, 1 J. & H. 278.

[5] *Bird* v. *Relph*, 4 B. & Ad. 826; 2 A. & E. 773.

[6] *Duke of St Albans* v. *Skipwith*, 8 Beav. 354.

[7] *Hoskins* v. *Fetherstone*, 2 Bro. C. C. 52.

[8] 4 D. & J. 414.

CHAP. 1. Sect. 9.

Holden v. *Weekes*,[9] Wood, V.-C. held that a patron could not claim an account and investment of the produce of past waste as of right, but the dictum of Lord Hardwicke, upon which that decision was based, may perhaps have meant only that the patron could not have such an account for his own benefit.[1] At all events, on a proper application, the Court would direct timber growing on glebe-land to be cut and the produce applied for the benefit of the living.[2]

School-house in churchyard.

In an Irish case[3] it was said that the Court of Chancery had no jurisdiction to interfere at the instance of a parishioner to restrain the incumbent from erecting a schoolhouse in the churchyard. Stress was laid in the judgment upon the facts that 177 heads of families wished the school to be erected, and were unable to procure a site through the opposition of the plaintiff, who was

[9] 1 J. & H. 278.

[1] *Knight* v. *Moseley*, 1 Amb. 176; see *Bird* v. *Relph*, 4 B. & Ad. 826; 2 A. & E. 773; *Huntley* v. *Russell*, 13 Q. B. 572; 13 Jur. 837; 18 L. J. Q. B. 139; and *Bishop of Winchester* v. *Knight*, 1 P. W. 406.

[2] *Duke of Marlborough* v. *St. John*, 5 De G. & S. 179.

[3] *Earl Fitzwilliam* v. *Moore*, 3 Ir. Eq. 615; Flan. & Kel. 287.

the principal landowner in the parish, and supported a school already existing.

Altering the fittings of a church.

A churchwarden has been allowed under special circumstances to maintain a bill on behalf of himself and the parishioners, to restrain an incumbent from improperly altering the fittings of the church.[4]

Episcopal leases without impeachment of waste.

Two curious cases have arisen out of long episcopal leases made without impeachment of waste, in the reign of Edward VI., and therefore before the restraining statutes. In the *Bishop of Winchester* v. *Wolgar*,[5] the lease was of land, in the manor of Havant, in the county of Southampton, and is expressly stated to have been made with the confirmation of the dean and chapter. In the year 1629 the assignee of the lease was restrained from felling timber at the suit of the then bishop, "regard being had of the common weal, and the commodiousness of the said timber for the maintenance of the shipping; and for that if the Lord Bishop him-

[4] *Cardinall* v. *Molyneux*, 2 Giff. 535, on appeal, 4 L. T., N. S. 605; see *Woodman* v. *Robinson*, 2 Sim. N. S. 204; and as to right of burial, *Moreland* v. *Richardson*, 24 Beav. 33.

[5] 3 Swanst. 493; see Freem. 55, and compare *Smythe* v. *Smythe*, 2 Swanst. 251.

Chap. I. Sect.

self should commit any excessive waste or spoil of woods, the same ought to be prohibited or restrained by law." In the *Bishop of London* v. *Webb*,[6] the lessee, when there were yet about twenty years of the term to run, articled with some brickmakers to carry away the soil of about twenty acres to the depth of six feet. Lord Macclesfield said, that this was within the principle of *Lord Barnard's Case*,[7] and that the lessee should not destroy the field to the ruin of the inheritance of the Church. It is not, however, easy to see how the principle there referred to can be applied to a contract for a pecuniary consideration.

Recent acts.

Various Acts have recently been passed, by which the management of episcopal and capitular estates will hereafter be regulated.[8]

[6] 1 P. W. 527 ; 2 Eq. Ab. 758, (decided 1718).

[7] *Vane* v. *Barnard*, 2 Vern. 738 ; Prec. Ch. 454 ; Gilb. Eq. Rep. 127 ; 1 Eq. Ab. 399 ; 1 Salk. 161.

[8] 14 & 15 Vict. c. 104 ; 17 & 18 Vict. c. 116 ; 22 & 23 Vict. c. 46 ; 23 & 24 Vict. c. 124 ; 24 & 25 Vict. c. 131.

CHAPTER II.

Chap. II.

NUISANCE.

SECT. 1.—NUISANCES IN GENERAL.

Sect. 1.

Nuisance.

Injuries to easements, and such injuries to natural rights of property as do not directly interfere with the possession of the soil, are nuisances.[1]

Public or private.

A nuisance may be of a public or of a private nature. This distinction was discussed in the case of *Soltau* v. *De Held*,[2] where an injunction was applied for to restrain the ringing of the bells of a Roman Catholic church close to the

[1] As to the refined distinction between direct and indirect injuries to real property, see *Reynolds* v. *Clarke*, 2 Ld. Raymond, 1399 ; *Scott* v. *Shepherd*, 1 Smith, Lead. Ca. ; *Scott* v. *Nelson*, 5 Ir. L. 207.

[2] 2 Sim. N. S. 133.

plaintiff's residence.[3] Kindersley, V.C., there said—"I conceive that to constitute a public nuisance, the thing must be such as in its nature or its consequences is a nuisance, an injury, or a damage, to all persons who come within the sphere of its operation, though it may be so in a greater degree to some than it is to others. For example, take the case of the operations of a manufactory, in the course of which operations volumes of noxious smoke or of poisonous effluvia are emitted. To all persons who are at all within the reach of those operations, it is more or less objectionable, more or less a nuisance in the popular sense of the term. It is true that to those who are nearer to it, it may be a greater nuisance, a greater inconvenience than it is to those who are more remote from it; but still to all who are at all within the reach of it, it is more or less a nuisance or an inconvenience. Take another ordinary case, perhaps the most ordinary case of a public nuisance, the stopping of the King's Highway, that is a nuisance to all who may have occasion to travel that highway. It may be a much greater nuisance to a person

[3] *Rex* v. *Lloyd*, 4 Esp. 200.

who has to travel it every day of his life, than it is to a person who has to travel it only once a year, or once in five years, but it is more or less a nuisance to every one who has occasion to use it. If, however, the thing complained of is such that it is a great nuisance to those who are more immediately within the sphere of its operations, but is no nuisance or inconvenience whatever, or is even advantageous or pleasurable to those who are more removed from it, then I conceive it does not come within the meaning of the term Public Nuisance.[4] The case before me is a case in point."[5]

Jurisdiction.

Courts of equity interfere in cases as well of private as of public nuisance, in the first at the suit of the party injured, in the second at the suit of the Attorney-General, both to restrain the exercise of a nuisance, and to prevent one from being created.[6] An individual, however, may sue in respect of a public nuisance from which he sustains special damage, either alone,[7] or with the

[4] See *Squire* v. *Campbell*, 1 My. & Cr. 486.

[5] See *Martin* v. *Nutkin*, 2 P. W. 266.

[6] Mitford Pleadings, 4th edit. p. 144.

[7] *Iveson* v. *Moor*, Com. 58; *Baines* v. *Baker*, 1 Amb. 158; 3 Atk. 750; *Crowder* v. *Tinkler*, 19 Ves. 617; *Spencer* v.

CHAP. II. Sect. 1.

Attorney-General, by information and bill.[8] In the *Attorney-General* v. *The United Kingdom Electric Telegraph Company*,[9] the defendants dug a trench along a public footpath. The Attorney-General filed an information to restrain the public nuisance, at the relation of the owner of the soil, who also preferred a bill complaining of the same act as a trespass.

Owners of neighbouring tenements.

Owners of neighbouring tenements ought not to join as co-plaintiffs in a suit to restrain an act which is a separate nuisance to each of them.[1]

Circumstances under which a court of equity will interfere.

A Court of equity will only interfere in a case of nuisance where the thing complained of is a nuisance at law,[2] and whether the nuisance be

London and Birmingham Railway Company, 8 Sim. 193; *Sampson* v. *Smith*, 8 Sim. 272; *Semple* v. *London and Birmingham Railway Company*, 1 Rlwy. Ca. 480; *Haines* v. *Taylor*, 10 Beav. 75; 2 Phil. 209; *Walter* v. *Selfe*, 4 De G. & S. 315; *Soltau* v. *De Held*, 2 Sim. N. S. 133; *Rose* v. *Groves*, 6 Scott, N. C. 645; see *Illingworth* v. *Manchester and Leeds Railway Company*, 2 Rlwy. Ca. 187.

[8] *Attorney-General* v. *Johnson*, 2 Wils. C. C. 87; *Attorney-General* v. *Forbes*, 2 Myl. & Cr. 123; *Attorney-General* v. *The Sheffield Gas Consumers' Company*, 3 D. M. G. 304; *Attorney-General* v. *The Luton Board of Health*, 2 Jur. N. S. 180.

[9] 10 W. R. 167.

[1] *Hudson* v. *Maddison*, 12 Sim. 416; *Pollock* v. *Lester*, 11 Hare, 266. The author apprehends that, notwithstanding these cases, the practice is not uncommon, see post, p. 115.

[2] *Soltau* v. *De Held*, 2 Sim. N. S. 133; *Semple* v. *London and*

public[3] or private[4] a judgment at law should in general be obtained before the hearing.

Right must be established at law.

It was said by Lord Kingsdown, in *Broadbent* v. *Imperial Gas Company*,[5] "The rule I take to be clearly this; if a plaintiff applies for an injunction to restrain a violation of a common law right, if either the existence of the right or the fact of its violation be disputed,[6] he must establish that right at law; but when he has established his right at law, I apprehend that, unless there be something special in the case, he is entitled, as of course, to an injunction to prevent a recurrence of that violation." But the Court of Chancery, in its discretion, may decide any

Court of Chancery may decide questions of law or fact.

Birmingham Railway Company, 9 Sim. 209; 1 Rlwy. Ca. 120; *Attorney-General* v. *London and Southampton Railway Company*, 9 Sim. 78; 1 Rlwy. Ca. 283; *Attorney-General* v. *Manchester and Leeds Railway Company*, 1 Rlwy. Ca. 436.

[3] *Attorney-General* v. *Cleaver*, 18 Ves. 211; *Attorney-General* v. *Sheffield Gas Consumers' Company*, 3 D. M. G. 304. As to purprestures or encroachments on the Queen's soil, see Mit. Pl., 4th edit. p. 145.

[4] *Anon.*, 2 Ves. S. 414; *Chalk* v. *Wyatt*, 3 Mer. 688; *Elmhirst* v. *Spencer*, 2 Mac. & Gor. 45; *Broadbent* v. *Imperial Gas Company*, 7 D. M. G. 436; 7 H. L. C. 600; *White* v. *Cohen*, 1 Dr. 312. See *Davies* v. *Marshall*, 1 Dr. & Sm. 557; *Gale* v. *Abbott*, V. C. K. 21st July, 1862.

[5] 7 H. L. C. 612; cf. *Attorney-General* v. *Nichol*, 16 Ves. 338; 3 Mer. 687.

[6] *Potts* v. *Levy*, 2 Dr. 272.

CHAP. II. Sect. 1. Interlocutory injunction.

questions of law or fact if the plaintiff and defendant both desire it.[7] An interlocutory injunction will, of course, be granted before the trial at law, where there is danger of irreparable mischief being done in the meantime.[8]

Damages an inadequate compensation.

The observations of Lord Kingsdown were probably not intended to abrogate the old rule that the Court of Chancery will not interfere where damages would be an adequate compensation. That was distinctly laid down by Lord Eldon in a case of darkening windows.[9] Lord Eldon there said:—"The foundation of this jurisdiction interfering by injunction is that head of mischief alluded to by Lord Hardwicke, that sort of natural injury to the comfort of the existence of those who dwell in the neighbouring house, requiring the application of a power to prevent as well as remedy an evil for which damages more or less would be given in an action at law. The position of the building, whether opposite, at right angles, or oblique, is not mate-

[7] *Walter* v. *Selfe*, 4 De G. & Sm. 315; 15 Jur. 418; on appeal, 19 L. T. 308; qy. as to prejudicing the right of appeal. And see *Ennor* v. *Barwell*, 2 Giff. 410; on appeal, 4 L. T. N. S. 597.

[8] *Earl of Ripon* v. *Hobart*, 3 My. & K. 169, &c., &c.

[9] *Attorney-General* v. *Nichol*, 16 Ves. 338; 3 Mer. 687.

rial. The question is, whether the effect is such an obstruction as the party has no right to erect, and cannot erect without those mischievous consequences which upon equitable principles should be not only compensated by damages, but prevented by injunction." Lord Eldon, therefore, in that case clearly refers the jurisdiction of the Court to the extent of the injury, and to the preventive power of the Court of Chancery, as being superior to the remedy which can be obtained at law.

Attorney-General v. Sheffield Gas Consumers' Company.

In *Attorney-General* v. *The Sheffield Gas Consumers' Company*,[1] Lord Justice Turner, after citing the above passage, continued—"But it is said, however that may be in a case of private nuisance, which was the case to which Lord Eldon was addressing himself in the case of the *Attorney-General* v. *Nichol*, it is different in the case of a public nuisance, and that it is the duty of this Court to interfere in all cases of public nuisance. The argument is put thus: it is said that no injury or inconvenience which is merely trifling would amount to a nuisance at law, that the very fact of there being a nuisance at law imports that

[1] 3 D. M. G. 319.

Chap. II.
Sect. 1.

the injury is great, and the inconvenience considerable, and, therefore, it is said that the interference of this Court must take place whenever there is a nuisance at law. I confess, however, that looking at the principles on which, as I apprehend, this Court interferes, it does not appear to me that there can be any sound distinction between cases of private and public nuisances. It is not on the ground of any criminal offence committed, or for the purpose of giving a better remedy in the case of a criminal offence, that this Court is or can be called on to interfere. It is on the ground of injury to property that the jurisdiction of this Court must rest; and taking it to rest upon that ground, the only distinction which seems to me to exist between cases of public nuisance and private nuisance is this, that in cases of private nuisance the injury is to individual property, and in cases of public nuisance the injury is to the property of mankind.

"I think, therefore, that the same principle must govern the question as to the iuterference of the Court, whether the case be one of private or of public nuisauce. What then is the principle by which the Court ought to be governed? I take it to be this: whether the extent of the damage and injury be such that the law will not afford an adequate and sufficient remedy. The same principle which governs the Court in other cases, in which its jurisdiction is more generally applied, seems to me to apply in such cases as the present. In cases of specific performance the jurisdiction of this Court is founded on the inadequacy of the remedy at law. If the specific performance of a covenant be asked, it is not every covenant which this Court will perform, but such covenants only as cannot be adequately compensated in damages.[2] So again, in cases of trespass, it is not every trespass against which this Court will enjoin; but such trespasses as are, or are assumed to be, irremediable, or at all events material; and so I take it to be in cases of nuisances."[3]

Application to particular state of facts.

Although the principle thus laid down is very clear, the case which we are now considering shows the difficulty which may sometimes arise in applying it to a particular state of facts. The

[2] See *Tipping* v. *Eckersley*, 2 K. & J. 270; and ante, p. 65.

[3] *Wynstanley* v. *Lee*, 2 Swanst. 333; *Soltau* v. *De Held*, 2 Sim. N. S. 158; *Wood* v. *Sutcliffe*, 2 Sim. N. S. 168; *Bostock* v. *North Staffordshire Railway Company*, 5 De G. & Sm. 584; *Rochdale Canal Company* v. *King*, 2 Sim. N. S. 78.

defendants were a gas company who had no authority to break up the roads, and an information and bill was filed seeking to restrain them from so doing, a rival gas company being relators and plaintiffs. The Court differed in opinion. Turner, L. J., considered that the injunction ought not to issue, on the ground that the inconvenience occasioned by laying down the pipes would only last for two or three days, and further said—"As to the continual taking up of the pavement consequent on these pipes having been laid down, that inconvenience will also, as it appears to me, be partial and temporary only. It will be an inconvenience occurring from time to time in different parts of the town, and not an injury affecting the general body of the inhabitants to any such extent as ought, in my opinion, to induce the interference of this Court. It is not to be left out of consideration in determining this question, that to some extent the law has provided a remedy in respect of these inconveniences. There is some remedy under the Highway Act; and there are boards of surveyors having control of the streets who, it is to be remembered, concur in these measures being taken; and as to any injury which private individuals may sustain, the law is open to them by actions on the case." On the other hand the Lord Justice K. Bruce took the following somewhat different view. "It has been argued that the annoyance (if any) felt, and possible to be feared, must be small, slight, and unfit for this Court's interference. But the frequent recurrence for ever, or during a period probably long and unascertainable, of an annoyance slight in itself (slight I mean if occurring but upon a single occasion, or occurring only at very rare intervals), may much interfere with the reasonable convenience and comfort of life. Upon the evidence now before us it is, I think, reasonable to believe that during a period probably long and unascertainable, the defendant's proceedings under consideration, unless judicially prevented, will unlawfully be of frequent recurrence, and will unlawfully create, from time to time, often inconvenience to persons who as travellers or passengers may have occasion to use the public streets and highways in Sheffield, to shopkeepers and other inhabitants of the town, and to the plaintiffs; nor, if we now refused an injunction, can it reasonably, I think, be denied that in respect of these unlawful proceedings, actual and intended, redress, remedy, or punishment may from time to time, for many years to come, be sought at law criminally and civilly, as well summarily as otherwise, to a very inconvenient and burthensome extent of diversified litigation, at the instance of a variety of persons." And finally Lord Cranworth, L. C., said—"I am of opinion that no case is made out for an injunction. With reference to the future evil of tearing up the streets for the purpose of repairs and the possibility of accidents, I can only say here that I must deal with those considerations exactly in the same way, and inquire whether there is such a probability of serious injury as would induce this Court to interfere? Everybody who has lived in this town has probably lived in a house where there have been gas pipes running along the front of it. Speaking for myself, I can say that I have experienced it for some twenty or thirty years and more, and I have never found any nuisance from such a source. I do not mean to say that evils may not occasionally occur, but I think that the interests of mankind require that these things should be disregarded. I concur, therefore, with

Lord Justice Turner, in thinking that this bill and information ought to be dismissed, though I entirely concur with both the Lords Justices that nothing should be said about the costs."

Restoring enjoyment of right.

Moreover the Court will not interfere unless the surrounding circumstances leave it practicable to restore the enjoyment of the right.[4]

Time at which application should be made.

The application should not be made until an actual nuisance has been committed, or at all events until it is quite clear that the works going on will inevitably result in a nuisance;[5] but due diligence must then be used, and a man may so encourage another in the erection of a nuisance as to render himself liable to be restrained from recovering damages at law for such nuisance when completed.[6]

Nuisance by public functionaries.

When public functionaries go beyond the line of their authority and assume a power over property which the law does not give, they are considered as no longer acting under the autho-

[4] *Wood* v. *Sutcliffe*, 2 Sim. N. S. 163.

[5] *Haines* v. *Taylor*, 10 Beav. 75; 2 Phil. 209; *Wicks* v. *Hunt*, J. 372; see *Elwell* v. *Crowther*, 10 W. R. 615; 6 L. T. N. S. 596.

[6] *Williams* v. *Earl of Jersey*, Cr. & Ph. 91; *Davies* v. *Marshall*, 1 Dr. & S. 557; *Jones* v. *The Royal Canal Company*, 2 Moll. 319.

CHAP. II. Sect. 1.

rity of their commission, and are treated, whether they are a corporation or individuals, merely as persons dealing with property illegally.[7] Bills to restrain nuisances have been entertained against the following functionaries:—Commissioners of Sewers;[8] Conservators of the Thames;[9] Justices of the Peace;[1] Drainage Commissioners;[2] Commissioners of Woods and Forests;[3] Boards of Health;[4] Trustees of Turnpike Roads.[5]

7 *Frewin* v. *Lewis*, 4 My. & Cr. 255; *Birley* v. *Constables of Chorlton-upon-Medlock*, 3 Beav. 499.

8 *Box* v. *Allen*, 1 Dick. 49; *Kerrison* v. *Sparrow*, 19 Ves. 449.

9 *Attorney-General* v. *Johnson*, 2 Wils. C. C. 87.

1 *Attorney-General* v. *Forbes*, 2 Myl. & Cr. 123.

2 *Earl of Ripon* v. *Hobart*, 3 Myl. & K. 169; *Dawson* v. *Paver*, 5 Hare, 415.

3 *Squire* v. *Campbell*, 1 Myl. & Cr. 459.

4 *Oldaker* v. *Hunt*, 6 D. M. G. 376; 3 Eq. Rep. 671; *Attorney-General* v. *The Luton Board of Health*, 2 Jur. N. S. 160; *Tinkler* v. *The Wandsworth Board of Health*, 6 W. R. 50, 390; *Manchester, Sheffield, and Lincolnshire Railway Company* v. *The Worksop Board of Health*, 23 Beav. 198; *Attorney-General* v. *The Borough of Birmingham*, 4 K. & J. 528; Seton on Decrees, 3rd edit. 894.

5 *Weeks* v. *Heward*, 10 W. R. 557.

Sect. 2.—NUISANCES TO DWELLING-HOUSES.

Jurisdiction.

In the case of nuisance to dwelling-houses, the jurisdiction is founded on the injury to the ordinary comfort,[6] or safety[7] of the inmates. The bill is usually brought by the occupier; but when the house is unoccupied, the owner may sue,[8] and he may possibly be allowed to do so in cases where an action would lie by reason of the nuisance being an injury to the reversion.[9]

Who may sue in equity.

When landlord may be sued at law for a nuisance by his tenant.

With respect to a landlord's liability to be sued for a nuisance, the rule at law[1] is, "If a landlord lets premises not in themselves a nuisance, but which may or may not be used

[6] *Attorney-General* v. *Nichol*, 16 Ves. 338; 1 Mer. 687; *Attorney-General* v. *Cleaver*, 18 Ves. 210; *Wynstanley* v. *Lee*, 2 Swanst. 333; *Walter* v. *Selfe*, 4 De G. & Sm. 315; *Soltau* v. *De Held*, 2 Sim. N. S. 133.

[7] *Crowder* v. *Tinkler*, 19 Ves. 617; see *Baines* v. *Baker*, 3 Atk. 750; 1 Amb. 158; *City of London* v. *Bolt*, 5 Ves. 128.

[8] *Wilson* v. *Townend*, 1 Dr. & S. 324; *Cleeve* v. *Mahany*, 9 W. R. 881.

[9] See and compare *White* v. *Cohen*, 1 Dr. 312; and *Wilson* v. *Townend*, 1 Dr. & S. 329; *Metropolitan Association* v. *Petch*, 5 C. B. N. S. 504; 27 L. J. C. P. 330.

[1] *Rich* v. *Basterfield*, 4 C. B. 783; *Todd* v. *Flight*, 9 C. B. N. S. 377.

Chap. II. Sect. 2.

by the tenant so as to become a nuisance, and it is entirely at the option of the tenant so to use them or not, and the landlord receives the same benefit whether they are so used or not, the landlord cannot be made responsible for the acts of the tenant."

Windows.

One of the nuisances to dwelling-houses which most frequently calls for the interference of the Court, is the interruption by erections on one man's land of the access of light and air to the windows of his neighbours.[2] Lord Eldon said,[3] "There is little doubt that this Court will not interfere upon every degree of darkening ancient lights and windows. There are many obvious cases of new buildings, darkening those opposite to them, but not in such a degree than an injunction could be maintained, or an action upon the case; which, however, might be main-

[2] *Bateman* v. *Johnson*, FitzGibbon, 106; *Ryder* v. *Bentham*, 1 Ves. S. 543; *Wynstanley* v. *Lee*, 2 Swanst. 333; *Sutton* v. *Montfort*, 4 Sim. 559; *Back* v. *Stacey*, 2 Russ. 121; *Beardmer* v. *London and North Western Railway Company*, 5 Rlwy. Ca. 728; see, under C. L. P. Act, *Jessel* v. *Chaplin*, 2 Jur. N. S. 931.

[3] *Attorney-General* v. *Nichol*, 16 Ves. 338; cf. observations of Lord Kingsdown (cited ante), in *Broadbent* v. *Imperial Gas Company*, 7 H. L. C. 612.

tained in many cases which would not support an injunction." In *Smith* v. *Elger*,[4] where a building had been erected at a distance of thirty feet from the plaintiff's windows, and not more than half the height of the plaintiff's house, it was doubted whether the Court would interfere even if it was a legal nuisance. In an early case,[5] a wall built at a distance of only seventeen feet from an ancient window was allowed to remain.

Shutting out a prospect.

The shutting out of a pleasant prospect is no ground of interference.[6] And conversely an invasion of privacy by the opening of a new window in a neighbour's house, gives no right of suit or action[7] (unless it be in breach of an agreement[8]); the remedy is to block the new window up.

Invasion of privacy.

Right to new windows from agreement or severance.

The right to the passage of light to new windows may of course be given by express agree-

[4] 3 Jur. 790.

[5] *Fishmongers' Company* v. *East India Company*, 1 Dick. 165; see *Radcliffe* v. *Duke of Portland*, V. C. S., 10 W. R. 687.

[6] *Aldred's Case*, 9 Rep. 58a; *Attorney-General* v. *Doughty*, 2 Ves. S. 453; *Fishmongers' Company* v. *East India Company*, 1 Dick. 163; *Attorney-General* v. *Bentham*, 1 Dick. 277; *Squire* v. *Campbell*, 1 My. & Cr. 486; *Bathurst* v. *Burden*, 2 Bro. C. C. 64; see *Piggott* v. *Stratton*, J. 359, 1 D. F. J. 33.

[7] *Chandler* v. *Thompson*, 3 Camp. 80; *Turner* v. *Spooner*, 1 Dr. & Sm. 467.

[8] *Lady Andover* v. *Robertson*, 26 L. T. 23.

Chap. II. Sect. 2.

ment;[9] it may also arise from privity of title. Thus, where a man erected a house on his own lands, and then sold the house to one, and afterwards the land adjoining to another, it was resolved that as the builder himself could not stop the lights, as that would be to derogate from his own grant, so neither could any person claiming under him.[1] And when a man was known to have taken certain premises for the purpose of carrying on a trade especially requiring light, it was said that the landlord would not be allowed to diminish the light in the slightest degree.[2]

Right of the grantee.

This principle was generalised in *Ewart* v. *Cochrane*,[3] where Campbell, L. C., said, "I consider the law of Scotland, as well as the law of

[9] *Morris* v. *Lessees of Lord Berkeley*, 2 Ves. S. 452 ; *Attorney-General* v. *Doughty*, 2 Ves. S. 453 ; *East India Company* v. *Vincent*, 2 Atk. 83.

[1] *Palmer* v. *Fletcher*, 1 Lev. 122 ; 1 Sid. 167, 227 ; *Cox* v. *Matthews*, 1 Vent. 237 ; *Roswell* v. *Pryor*, 12 Mod. 635 ; 2 Salk. 460 ; 1 Ld. Ray. 713 ; *Coutts* v. *Gorham*, 1 Moo. & Mal. 396 ; *Blanchard* v. *Bridges*, 4 A. & E. 176 ; *Davies* v. *Marshall*, 1 Dr. & Sm. 557 ; see *Alston* v. *Grant*, 3 E. & B. 128.

[2] *Hertz* v. *Union Bank of London*, 24 L. T. 137, 186 ; *Fox* v. *Pursell*, 3 Sm. & G. 242 ; *Radcliffe* v. *Duke of Portland*, 10 W. R. 687.

[3] 4 Macq. 117 ; *Pyer* v. *Carter*, 1 H. & N. 916 ; *Caledonian Railway Company* v. *Sprot*, 2 Macq. 449 ; and see *post*, p. 152.

England, to be, that when two properties are possessed by the same owner, and there has been a severance made of part from the other, anything which was used, and was necessary for the comfortable enjoyment of that part of the property which is granted, shall be considered to follow from the grant if there be the usual words in the conveyance. I do not know whether the usual words are essentially necessary, but where there are the usual words, I cannot doubt that that is the law."

Right of the grantor.

A more difficult question is, whether easements used for the enjoyment of the part of the property which is retained can be considered to be reserved out of the grant, in opposition to the usual maxim, that a grant is to be construed most strongly against the grantor. It is settled that a reservation of easements of necessity can be so implied,[4] but there is considerable difficulty respecting lights.[5]

Easements of necessity.

In *Palmer* v. *Fletcher*,[6] Kelynge, J., said,

[4] *Pennington* v. *Galland*, 9 Exch. 1; *Richards* v. *Rose*, 9 Exch. 220; *Pearson* v. *Spencer*, 1 B. & S. 571; *Dugdale* v. *Robertson*, 3 K. & J. 695; and see *post*, p. 152.

[5] "Habitare potest et ædibus obscuratis," Dig. Lib. viii. Tit. ii. § x.

[6] 1 Lev. 122; 1 Sid. 167, 227.

CHAP. II. Sect. 2.

"Suppose the land had been sold first and the house after, the vendee of the land might stop the lights." Twysden, J., to the contrary said, "Whether the land be sold first or afterwards, the vendee of the land cannot stop the lights of the house in the hands of the vendor or his assignees." The authorities in favour of either opinion are collected below.[7]

Houses built as part of the same plan.

In *Compton* v. *Richards*,[8] two houses were built by the same proprietor about the same time as part of the plan of a new crescent, and were sold in an unfinished state at the same sale to different persons; the openings which were intended to be supplied with windows being sufficiently visible;[9] upon these facts a con-

[7] For opinion of Kelynge, J., *Tenant* v. *Goldwin*, 2 Ld. Raymond, 1093; *White* v. *Bass*, 5 L. T. N. S. 843. For opinion of Twysden, J., *Riviere* v. *Bower*, Ry. & Moo. 24; *Crook* v. *Wilson*, 3 W. R. 378; Gale on Easements, 3rd edit. p. 82. The fact that the windows are more than 20 years old will not raise the presumption of a lost agreement or entitle the owner to the benefit of Lord Tenterden's Act, *Harbidge* v. *Warwick*, 3 Exch. 552. It has been urged that to deprive a grantee of the land, of the right of building, is as much a derogation from the grant, as it is in the converse case to deprive a grantee of the house of the access of light and air. Gibbon's Law of Dilapidations and Nuisances, 377.

[8] 1 Price, 27; see *Swansborough* v. *Coventry*, 9 Bing. 305; *Richard* v. *Rose*, 9 Exch. 218; *Pyer* v. *Carter*, 26 L. J. Exch. 258

[9] *Glave* v. *Harding*, 27 L. J. Exch. 286.

dition was implied that nothing should afterwards be done by either purchaser, by which his neighbour's windows might be obstructed.

Right to ancient windows.

There are three modes of establishing a title to an easement by user, (1) By sufficient evidence of enjoyment during the whole time of legal memory; (2) By proof of enjoyment for such time and under such circumstances as will justify the finding of a lost grant or agreement since the commencement of legal memory; (3) By proof of enjoyment for such time and under such circumstances as will satisfy the provisions of Lord Tenterden's Act.[1]

Immemorial enjoyment.

The first mode of proof does not require that the evidence should be carried back to the accession of Richard I. (1189), which has long been fixed as the date at which legal memory begins, because evidence of enjoyment for a shorter time is sufficient to raise a presumption of enjoyment for the whole period. Thus it was said by Parke, B., in *Jenkins* v. *Harvey*,[2] "A

[1] 2 & 3 Will. 4, c. 71.

[2] 1 Cr. M. & R. 894; 2 Cr. M. & R. 393; 5 Tyr. 326; *Bury* v. *Pope*, Cro. Eliz. 118; *Blewitt* v. *Tregonning*, 3 A. & E. 556; *Webb* v. *Bird*, 10 C. B. N. S. 268, in error, 8 Jur. N. S. 621; *O'Neill* v. *Allen*, 9 Ir. C. L. 132.

CHAP. II. Sect. 2.

clear usage from the year 1777 for a lessee to receive certain tolls, coupled with the proof of its being a valuable right in 1752, was amply sufficient to warrant the jury in presuming the practice to have existed time out of mind." A

Prescription.

title made out in this manner is a title by Prescription, in the strict sense of the word; but the term is frequently used of titles made out in the 2nd and 3rd modes. Prescription supposes a deed or document creating the right, to have existed before the time of legal memory;[3] and the title is conclusively defeated if the commencement of the enjoyment can be shown to have been subsequent to that epoch.

Presumption of lost grant or agreement.

In order to prevent an old title from failing in this manner, the Courts introduced the fiction, which is the basis of the second mode of proof. We have already pointed out that no action lies against a man for opening a new window which overlooks his neighbour's lands; and conse-

Light a negative easement.

quently light is an exception to the general rule that the exercise of an acquired easement must, in the first instance, have been illegal; for this

[3] *Potter* v. *North*, 1 Vent. 387; Best on Presumptions, p. 89.

reason it is called a negative easement.[4] Now, in the case of affirmative easements, if the owner of the land over which they are being exercised brings no action, and takes no step to obstruct the acts of enjoyment for twenty years, his acquiescence gives rise to the presumption of a grant of the easement having been made and lost; and, by analogy to this doctrine, although the right of light perhaps does not lie in grant, and acts of enjoyment give no cause of action, yet if the owner of the neighbouring land allows the windows to remain unobstructed for twenty years, this is a sufficient foundation for the presumption of an agreement or covenant by him not to obstruct them.[5]

Extent of rights acquired by presumption of a lost grant or agreement.

No larger right, it would seem, can be acquired under this fiction than what some person in existence during the usage shown, or a little earlier, and able to resist it, was capable of

[4] Gale on Easements, 3rd edit. p. 18.

[5] *Cross* v. *Lewis*, 2 B. & C. 686; *Moore* v. *Rawson*, 3 B. & C. 332; *Penwarden* v. *Ching*, 1 Moo. & Mal. 400; *Stokoe* v. *Singers*, 8 E. & B. 31; *Webb* v. *Bird*, 10 C. B. N. S. 268, in error, 8 Jur. N. S. 621. The burden of a covenant not to build does not run with the land at law (*Spencer's Case*, 1 Smith, Lead. Ca.). As to equity see *Tulk* v. *Moxhay*, 2 Phil. 774.

CHAP. II. Sect. 2.

creating.[6] Thus, enjoyment adverse to a tenant for life or years,[7] or a rector,[8] will not bind the inheritance.

Lord Tenterden's Act.

The anomaly of requiring a jury to find the existence of a grant or agreement where, in all probability, no grant or agreement ever existed, led to Lord Tenterden's Act,[9] which was intended to answer the same purpose. The preamble is, "Whereas, the expression, 'Time immemorial, or, time whereof the memory of man runneth not to the contrary,' is now by the law of England in many cases considered to include and denote the whole period of time from the reign of King Richard the First, whereby the title to matters that have been long enjoyed is sometimes defeated by *showing the commencement of such*

[6] *Blewitt* v. *Tregonning*, 3 A. & E. 583; *Bright* v. *Walker*, 1 C. M. & R. 211; *Padwick* v. *Knight*, 22 L. J. Ex. 198; see *Tyler* v. *Wilkinson*, 4 Mason, 402; *Little* v. *Wingfield*, 11 Ir. C. L. 87.

[7] *Daniel* v. *North*, 11 East, 372. As to acquiescence by reversioner see *Gray* v. *Bond*, 2 Bro. & B. 667; *Rex* v. *Barr*, 4 Camp. 16; *Hanks* v. *Cribbin*, 7 Ir. C. L. 489; *Lincham* v. *Deeble*, 9 Ir. C. L. 309; 12 Ir. C. L. 1.

[8] *Barber* v. *Richardson*, 4 B. & Ald. 579. For plea of grant by a dean and chapter before the restraining statutes, *Blewitt* v. *Tregonning*, 3 A. & E. 556; and see *Sutton* v. *Lord Mountfort*, 4 Sim. 559.

[9] 2 & 3 Will. 4, c. 71.

enjoyment, which is in many cases productive of inconvenience and injustice; for remedy thereof be it enacted, &c."[1]

§ 3. Light.

The third section provides with regard to light, "That when the access and use of light to and for any dwelling-house, workshop, or other building, shall have been actually enjoyed therewith for the full period of twenty years without interruption, the right thereto shall be deemed absolute and indefeasible, any local usage or custom to the contrary notwithstanding, unless it shall appear that the same was enjoyed by some consent or agreement expressly made or given for that purpose by deed or writing."

Construction of Act.

Duration of interruption.

By the construction placed upon this section together with the fourth, it appears that there must be twenty years from the commencement of the right of enjoyment to the commencement of the suit, and that no interruption is to be considered as preventing the twenty years from

[1] The title by lost grant has not been taken away by this Act. "The jury may still find a grant to have been made, if they are satisfied that it was made in point of fact" (per Parke, B., *Bright* v. *Walker*, 1 C. M. & R. 222), but qu. whether the presumption of a grant may be made as before (*Blewitt* v. *Tregonning*, 3 A. & E. 556; *Webb* v. *Bird*, 10 C. B. N. S. 268; 8 Jur. N. S. 621; *Deeble* v. *Lincham*, 12 Ir. C. L. 1; *Wilson* v. *Stanley*, 12 Ir. C. L. 345).

CHAP. II. Sect. 2.

running, unless it has a duration of one year, so that if there has been an enjoyment for nineteen years and a fraction, and then an interruption takes place, the right may be established at the end of the twentieth year.[2]

Twenty years' enjoyment binding on the inheritance.

The statute makes twenty years' enjoyment of light without interruption binding upon the inheritance of the premises upon which the restriction is to be imposed, unless such user is had under some written consent. So that by negligence, or wilfully, a lessee may allow a valuable right to be acquired against his landlord's property; and it is difficult to say what remedy, if any, the landlord has.

Lessee of servient tenement.

It would probably be held that a right of light acquired by a tenant would enure to the benefit of the reversion; and questions may hereafter arise whether an interruption acquiesced in by a tenant, or a written consent accepted by him, would deprive the reversioner of the benefit of the statute.

Lessee of dominant tenement.

It has been decided that no title to an easement can be acquired under this statute against a lessee, except under circumstances which would give a valid right against the rever-

Right against owner of a particular estate.

[2] *Flight* v. *Thomas*, 11 A. & E. 695; 8 Cl. & F. 231.

sioner.[3] As twenty years' enjoyment of light gives such a right against a reversioner, it of course also gives a good title against a lessee. This was decided in *Frewen* v. *Phillips*,[4] where, in the case of two lessees holding under the same reversioner, it was held that the enjoyment by one of the access of light over the premises of the other for twenty years conferred on the lessee so enjoying the light an absolute right.

Rent not an interruption.

The demand and payment of rent for the use of light is not an interruption under this section, but it may prevent the enjoyment from being such as to satisfy the statute.[5]

Legal origin.

It is in general necessary that rights claimed under this statute should be such as might, by possibility, have had a legal origin,[6] but light may be an exception.

[3] *Bright* v. *Walker*, 1 C. M. & R. 220; *Wilson* v. *Stanley*, 12 Ir. C. L. 345.

[4] 11 C. B. N. S. 449; see Dart, V. & P., 3rd edit. pp. 246, 247.

[5] *Plasterers' Company* v. *Parish Clerks' Company*, 6 Exch. 630; see *Mayor of London* v. *Pewterers' Company*, 2 Moo. & Rob. 409. As to what will constitute an interruption within the meaning of this statute, see *Gale* v. *Abbott*, 10 W. R. 748, Dart, V. & P., 3rd edit. p. 248.

[6] *Rochdale Canal Company* v. *Radcliffe*, 18 Q. B. 287; *Mill* v. *New Forest Commissioners*, 18 C. B. 60; *National Manure Company* v. *Donald*, 4 H. & N. 8.

CHAP. II. Sect. 2.

Unity of possession.

Unity of possession of the dominant and servient tenements will prevent a statutory right from arising, unity of ownership being necessary to extinguish a similar right at common law.[7]

Custom of London.

When a title to light is made under the statute, an obstruction cannot be justified by the custom of London. But if the right exists only at the common law, the custom remains.[8]

Loss of right by blocking up window.

We have now to consider how the privilege of receiving light through a particular window may be lost. Where an ancient window had been blocked up with bricks and mortar for twenty years, Lord Ellenborough said that the case stood as if it had never existed;[9] but blocking windows for a less period than twenty years will not destroy the right, unless it be done so as to manifest an intention of permanently abandoning the right of using them, or so as to lead the neighbour to incur expense or loss, with reasonable belief that they had been permanently abandoned.[1]

7 *Onley* v. *Gardner*, 4 M. & W. 499 ; Co. Litt. 114 b ; Gale on Easements.

8 *Salters' Company* v. *Jay*, 3 Q. B. 109 ; *Truscott* v. *Merchant Taylors' Company*, 11 Exch. 855 ; see *Wynstanley* v. *Lee*, 2 Swanst. 333 ; *Fox* v. *Pursell*, 3 Sm. & G. 242.

9 *Lawrence* v. *Obee*, 3 Camp. 514.

1 *Stokoe* v. *Singers*, 8 E. & B. 31.

CHAP. II. Sect. 2. Loss of right by pulling down the building.

The right may also be lost by pulling down or altering the buildings in which the windows are placed. In *Moore* v. *Rawson*,[2] Littledale, J., said—"If a man pulls down a house and does not make any use of the land for two or three years or converts it into tillage, I think he may be taken to have abandoned all intention of rebuilding the house; and consequently that his right to the light has ceased. But if he builds upon the same site[3] and places windows in the same spot or does anything to show that he did not mean to convert the land to a different purpose, then his right would not cease." An owner who rebuilds or alters his house is of course not entitled to more light than before,[4] and the windows through which he receives it must be substantially in the former place, and be neither larger nor more numerous.[5] If it happens that the new windows are partly in the same positions as the old ones and partly not, such portions of the new apertures as were open

Effect of alterations.

[2] 3 B. & C. 332, 339; 2 C. & P. N. P. C. 466.

[3] *Fishmongers' Company* v. *East India Company*, 1 Dick. 163.

[4] *Marten* v. *Goble*, 1 Camp. 320; *Garrett* v. *Sharp*, 3 A. & E. 325.

[5] *Cherington* v. *Abney*, 2 Vern. 646; *East India Company* v. *Vincent*, 2 Atk. 283.

CHAP. II. Sect. 2.

before remain privileged.[6] But if there is no mode of obstructing the unprivileged portions alone, and the substituted lights are substantially different from the former ones in size or position, the owner of the servient tenement may obstruct the whole,[7] until the windows are restored to their former condition, when it seems, according to recent authorities, that the obstruction must be removed.[8]

Obstruction on the owner's premises.

When the owner of a house has removed an obstruction to light which had existed on his own premises for more than twenty years, it has been suggested that the adjoining owner may be entitled to erect an obstruction as great;[9] it is settled, however, that heavy sashes and frames

[6] *Luttrell's Case*, 4 Rep. 87 a; *Chandler* v. *Thompson*, 3 Camp. 80; *Garrett* v. *Sharpe*, 3 A. & E. 325; *Blanchard* v. *Bridges*, 4 A. & E. 176.

[7] *Cherington* v. *Abney*, 2 Vern. 646; *Renshaw* v. *Bean*, 18 Q. B. 112; *Wilson* v. *Townend*, 1 Dr. & S. 324; *Davies* v. *Marshall*, 1 Dr. & Sm. 557; *Turner* v. *Spooner*, 1 Dr. & Sm. 467; *Hutchinson* v. *Copestake*, 8 C. B. N. S. 102.

[8] *Caukwell* v. *Russell*, 26 L. J. Exch. 34; *Cooper* v. *Hubbuck*, 30 Beav. 160; *Jones* v. *Tapling*, 11 C. B. N. S. 283, in error not yet reported, now in H. L.; *Binckes* v. *Pash*, 11 C. B. N. S. 324.

[9] *Cotterill* v. *Griffiths*, 4 Esp. 69; *Arcedeckne* v. *Kelk*, 5 Jur. N. S. 114.

may be replaced by others of a lighter construction.[1]

Passage of air.

Windows which have the privilege of receiving light have also the privilege of receiving air, so that a neighbour may not obstruct them by a transparent screen or sky-light.[2] A prescription for the access of currents of air for trade purposes, such as drying timber[3] or serving a windmill,[4] can only be established (if at all) by such evidence as would justify the jury in finding that the enjoyment had existed from time immemorial. No action lies against a person for appropriating the benefit of such currents, and it is impossible to obstruct them without an unreasonable amount of labour and expense; for these reasons no presumption can be made of a lost agreement not to obstruct, and Lord Tenterden's Act does not apply to any negative easement except light.[5]

rickburning.

Differences of opinion have existed as to the

[1] *Chandler* v. *Thompson*, 3 Camp. 80; *Turner* v. *Spooner*, 1 Dr. & Sm. 467.

[2] *Aldred's Case*, 9 Rep. 58 b; *Radcliffe* v. *Duke of Portland*, V.-C. S., 10 W. R. 687; *Gale* v. *Abbott*, V.-C. K., 10 W. R. 748.

[3] *Roberts* v. *Macord*, 1 Moo. & Rob. 230.

[4] *Webb* v. *Bird*, 10 C. B. N. S. 268, in error, 8 Jur. N. S. 621.

[5] *Harbidge* v. *Warwick*, 3 Exch. 557; *Webb* v. *Bird*, 10 C. B. N. S. 268, in error, 8 Jur. N. S. 621.

Chap. II. Sect. 2.

manner and place in which brickburning may be carried on so as not to be a legal nuisance. The earliest case upon the subject seems to be *The Duke of Grafton* v. *Hilliard.*[6] The defendants there had entered into articles of agreement for a ninety-four years' lease of a certain field called Brickfield, part of a farm called Hay Hill farm in the parish of St. George, Hanover Square; there was brick-earth upon part of the ground, which the defendants agreed by their articles not to burn except between the 1st of July and the last day of August. Lord Hardwicke refused on an interlocutory motion to restrain them from burning this earth into bricks upon the land, observing, according to Lord Eldon's note, that the manufacture of bricks, though near the habitations of men, if carried on for the purpose of making habitations for them, is not a public nuisance. By the report in Ambler, Lord Hardwicke dwelt upon the fact that if it should appear at the hearing that it was no nuisance, he would be unable to make the defendants amends, as their time for burning would

Duke of Grafton v. Hilliard.

Clay of the land.

Burning, temporary.

Lord Eldon's note.

Report in Ambler.

[6] 4 De G. & Sm. 326; 15 Jur. 418 n.; *Attorney-General* v. *Cleaver*, 18 Ves. 219; 1 Amb. 159; *Walter* v. *Selfe*, 4 De G. & Sm. 324; 19 L. T. 308.

Lord St. Leonards' note.

have expired. In *Walter* v. *Selfe*,[7] Lord St. Leonards stated that he had a MS. note from which he was induced to think that the decision went upon the fact that although there might be a nuisance, yet no nuisance was proved to exist. There were several plaintiffs, and the kiln was at the distance of sixty yards from the house of the nearest. We next come to *Barwell* v. *Brooks*.[8] An *exparte* injunction had been granted to restrain the defendants from burning bricks on their own land, within 200 yards of the plaintiff's property, called East Cowes Castle, which he had recently purchased of Lord Shannon. On a motion to dissolve, made on the 27th April, 1843, the defendant's affidavits stated that he had bought his land at a high price (not apparently from Lord Shannon or any person connected in title with him), for the purpose of a building speculation, that the bricks would not be burned in the particular situation which gave rise to the complaint for more than a few months, that an old kiln existed at the same place, and that the plaintiff's real object was to impede the defendant's specu-

Barwell v. *Brooks*.

7 19 L. T. 308.

8 1 L. T. 75-454 ; 15 Jur. 418 *n*.

lation. The defendant said that he had taken precautions to avoid unnecessary inconvenience to the plaintiff, and that the building scheme had been propounded and the plan made known to the plaintiff previously to his purchase, which he had made at a low price. The plaintiff averred that the bricks which had formerly been burned on defendant's property had been burned in a different and less objectionable place. The Vice-Chancellor of England held that the injunction ought to be dissolved, saying that the defendant by his answer stated that after he had made his purchase he communicated to Lord Shannon, then the owner of the plaintiff's mansion, the objects with which the farm had been bought, and he at once circulated a printed plan of his scheme of building upon it, in which was stated the advantage of getting brick-earth upon the estate. That he then called the farm East Cowes Park, which ceased to be used as a farm, but was laid out as building land. That at the time of the plaintiff's purchase he knew of the defendant's circular, and the plan of building and brickmaking was shown to him. None of these circumstances were mentioned in the bill. That was indefensible, for had

Notice.

those facts appeared in the bill, the injunction would not have been granted. By this suppression of facts, the defendant had misconducted himself towards the Court. An injunction is only granted from necessity, for *prima facie* it is unjust, and all that had been disclosed by the answer should have been stated. He did not think the defendant had unfairly stated in his answer that the brickburning would be temporary, because it was quite obvious that it would only last until the ground had been built upon. Neither was the plaintiff quite fair in the matter of the plan. The injunction was dissolved. The plaintiff then filed amended and supplemental bills denying notice and acquiescence, and renewed his application for an injunction. The points discussed were: 1. Whether there had been acquiescence? 2. Whether brickburning was a nuisance? 3. Whether a Court of equity would restrain a qualified use of it for the temporary purpose of building? There is no report of the judgment, but the injunction was granted as to a particular piece of land specified in the order. This order and a subsequent order of committal for a breach of it were carried by appeal to Lord Lyndhurst, when by agreement

Burning, temporary.

Chap. II. Sect. 2.

the injunction was made perpetual, and it was referred to Mr. Swanston to award compensation and costs. The clay burned seems to have been clay of the same land, but it is not clearly so stated.

Clay of the land.

Walter v. *Selfe.*

In *Walter* v. *Selfe*,[9] the kiln was situated about forty-eight yards from the plaintiff's house, and the evidence established that the comfort of the occupier was materially interfered with. The earth burned was of the clay of the land. Both parties asking the Court to decide without the intervention of a Court of law, the injunction was granted. An appeal was dismissed by Lord St. Leonards on the ground that the parties had bound themselves to abide by the decision of the Court below.[1]

Clay of the land.

Pollock v. *Lester.*

In *Pollock* v. *Lester*,[2] the defendant had a house and about an acre of ground on the opposite side of a high road to the houses of the plaintiffs, and at a distance of about sixty yards from the nearest of them. He pulled down the house and dug up the clay in order to

Clay of the land.

[9] 4 De G. & Sm. 315 ; 15 Jur. 418.

[1] 19 L. T. 308. This is not the present practice, *Ennor* v. *Barwell*, 4 L. T. N. S. 597.

[2] 11 Hare, 266.

burn it. An interlocutory injunction was granted on the undertaking of the defendants to proceed at law.

Hole v. Barlow.

The next case, *Hole* v. *Barlow*,[3] has been the subject of much comment. The plaintiff occupied a house in a newly formed road abutting upon a field belonging to the defendant, and upon which the defendant, preparatory to the building of certain houses thereon, had excavated the clay and converted it into bricks, which he carried to be placed in three clamps for burning near to the plaintiff's dwelling-house, one of them being within thirty feet of it. Two questions were left to the jury: 1. Was the place in which the bricks were burned a proper and convenient place for that purpose? and if not, 2. Was the nuisance such as to make the enjoyment of life and property uncomfortable? This direction was held to be correct. The jury returned a verdict for the defendants.

Clay of the land.

Bamford v. Turnley. Notice.

This was followed at Nisi Prius in *Bamford* v. *Turnley*,[4] where the plaintiff purchased a house on

[3] 4 C. B. N. S. 334; see *Stockport Water Works* v. *Potter*, 7 H. & N. 160; 7 Jur. N. S. 880.

[4] 2 Fos. & Fin. N. P. C. 231.

Chap. II. Sect. 2.

certain conditions and particulars of sale mentioning "that the adjoining land was fit for brickmaking." The defendant had bought the adjoining land of the same owner, and had commenced brickmaking thereon, accumulating heaps of ashes for the purpose, which he brought from other places, not working up only the brick-earth excavated on his own land. The jury were directed that if the spot was a proper and convenient spot, and the burning of the bricks was a reasonable use by the defendant of his own land, he was entitled so to use it, whether the plaintiff's comfort was interfered with or not. In the Exchequer Chamber,[5] however, it was ruled that as an offensive trade would be indictable as a public nuisance if carried on in a place where it greatly incommoded a multitude of persons, so it would be actionable if carried on in a place where it greatly incommoded an individual, however convenient the spot might be for the purposes of the trader. But it was said that acts necessary for the common use and occupation of lands and houses, such as burning weeds, emptying cesspools, making noises during repairs, &c., although very annoying to a neigh-

Clay brought from other places.

[5] 6 L. T. N. S. 721.

bour, might be lawfully done, if done in a reasonable way. *Hole* v. *Barlow* was expressly overruled.[6]

Notice.

It will be observed that in *Barwell* v. *Brooks*, *Hole* v. *Barlow*, and *Bamford* v. *Turnley*, the parties complaining of the nuisance had taken their houses knowing that the adjacent land was a likely place for brickmaking. But this alone would seem not to be sufficient to deprive them of their remedies for the nuisance either in equity or at law. Lord Tenterden, indeed, once ruled[7] that if a noxious trade is already established in a place remote from habitations, and public roads and houses are afterwards made and built so near to it that it becomes a nuisance, the party is still entitled to continue his trade. But this is probably not now law. At all events more recent cases[8] have decided that where a trade is at its commencement a nuisance to occupiers of houses in the neighbourhood, succeeding occupiers have an

Doctrine of coming to a nuisance.

6 See further as to brick-burning, *Cleeve* v. *Mahany*, V.-C. K., 9 W. R. 882; *Cavey* v. *Ledbitter*, 3 Fos. & Fin. N. P. C. 14; *Beardmore* v. *Tredwell*, V. C. S., compromised on appeal L. C. 26th July, 1862; *Steven* v. *Child*, N. P. 30th July, 1862.

7 *Rex* v. *Cross*, 2 C. & P. 483.

8 *Elliotson* v. *Feetham*, 2 Bing. N. C. 134; *Bliss* v. *Hall*, 4 Bing. N. C. 183.

Chap. II. Sect. 2.

equal right to complain of it, unless a right to carry it on has been acquired by prescription.

Various nuisances to dwelling-houses.

Other instances of nuisances to dwelling-houses where equitable relief has been sought, are soap-boiling,[8] coke ovens,[9] smoke of a steam engine,[1] gas works,[2] bell-ringing,[3] manufacture of gun-powder,[4] obstructing a chimney,[5] holding a regatta.[6]

A brewhouse is not necessarily a nuisance,[7] nor is a hospital for infectious diseases.[8]

For nuisances in general, see page 171, and see Appendix.

[8] *Attorney-General* v. *Cleaver*, 18 Ves. 211.

[9] *Semple* v. *London and Birmingham Railway Company*, 1 Rlwy. Ca. 120 ; see *King* v. *Dewey*, 5 Esp. 217.

[1] *Sampson* v. *Smith*, 8 Sim. 272.

[2] *Haines* v. *Taylor*, 10 Beav. 75 ; 2 Phil. 209 ; *Broadbent* v. *Imperial Gas Company*, 7 D. M. G. 436 ; 7 H. L. C. 600.

[3] *Soltau* v. *De Held*, 2 Sim. N. S. 133. See *Martin* v. *Nutkin*, 2 P. W. 266.

[4] *Crowder* v. *Tinkler*, 19 Ves. 617.

[5] *Hervey* v. *Smith*, 1 K. & J. 389.

[6] *Bostock* v. *North Staffordshire Railway Company*, 5 De G. & Sm. 584 ; 4 E. & B. 798.

[7] *Attorney-General* v. *Cleaver*, 18 Ves. 219 ; *Gorton* v. *Smart*, 1 S. & S. 66.

[8] *Baines* v. *Baker*, 1 Amb. 158 ; 3 Atk. 750 ; *Rex* v. *Sutton*, 4 Bur. 2116 ; *Rex* v. *Vantandillo*, 4 M. & S. 73.

Sect. 3.—NUISANCES RELATING TO WATER.

Sect. 3.

Riparian proprietors.

The right to the use of running water is thus stated in *Wright* v. *Howard.*[9] "*Primâ facie* the proprietor of each bank of a stream is the proprietor of half the land covered by the stream,[1] but there is no property in the water. Every proprietor has an equal right to use the water which flows in the stream, and consequently no proprietor can have the right to use the water to the prejudice of any other proprietor. Without the consent of the other proprietors who may be affected by his operations, no proprietor can either diminish the quantity of water which would otherwise descend to the proprietors below, nor throw the waters back upon the proprietors above."[2]

[9] 1 S. & S. 190; *Mason* v. *Hill*, 5 B. & Ad. 1. As to right of proprietors of land on the banks of a navigablo river, *Vooght* v. *Winch*, 2 B. & Ald. 662; *Proprietors of Medway Navigation* v. *Earl of Romney*, 4 L. T. N. S. 87. As to law of Lower Canada, see *Miner* v. *Gilmour*, 12 Moore, P. C. 131. And as to law of America, *Tyler* v. *Wilkinson*, 4 Mason, 397.

[1] Qy. whether riparian rights depend on the ownership of the soil of the stream, *Wood* v. *Waud*, 3 Exch. 748; *Lord* v. *Commissioners of Sidney*, 12 Moore, P. C. 473.

[2] As to backwater, see *Dawson* v. *Paver*, 5 Hare, 415; *Cooper* v. *Barber*, 3 Taunt. 99; *Saunders* v. *Newman*, 1 B. & Ald. 258; *National Manure Company* v. *Donald*, 4 H. & N. 8.

Chap. II. Sect. 3.

Excessive use. This must be understood of operations in excess of the reasonable use of the water which the law allows to every proprietor; and it may be remarked that in order to sustain an action, it is Actual damage. not necessary for the injured proprietor to show that he has incurred loss.[3]

Reasonable use. The question of what is considered in the English law to be a reasonable use of water by a riparian proprietor, was discussed in *Embrey* v. *Owen.*[4] The plantiffs were millowners, and the defendants, who were upper riparian proprietors, used from time to time to divert a part of the water for the purpose of irrigation, and then return it, some small amount being lost by absorption and evaporation. The Court abstained from laying down that it would in every case be deemed a lawful enjoyment of the water if it was again returned into the river with no other diminution than that so caused, but it was held that as the irrigation in the case then under consideration

[3] *Wood* v. *Waud,* 3 Exch. 748; *Embrey* v. *Owen,* 6 Exch. 353; *Sampson* v. *Hoddinott,* 1 C. B. N. S. 590; *Ferrand* v. *Corporation of Bradford,* 2 Jur. N. S. 175; *Tobin* v. *Stowell,* 9 Moore, P. C. 71; *Lord Norbury* v. *Kitchin,* N. P. 29th July, 1862.

[4] 6 Exch. 353; see further, on the subject of irrigation, *Sampson* v. *Hoddinott,* 1 C. B. N. S. 590.

took place not continuously, but only at intermittent periods, and no damage was done thereby to the working of the mill, and the diminution of the water was not perceptible to the eye, it was such a reasonable use of the water as not to be prohibited by law. The loss of water in this case was not more than 5 per cent.

Miner v. Gilmour

In *Miner* v. *Gilmour*,[5] Lord Kingsdown stated the law of Lower Canada, which he said did not materially differ on this question from that of England in the following terms: "By the general law applicable to running streams, every riparian proprietor has a right to what may be called the ordinary use of the water flowing past his land; for instance, to the reasonable use of the water for his domestic purposes and for his cattle,[6] and this without regard to the effect which such use may have in case of a deficiency upon proprietors lower down the stream. But further, he has a right to the use of it for any purpose, or what may be deemed the extraordinary use of it, provided that he does not thereby interfere with the rights of other proprietors either above or below

[5] 12 Moore, P. C. 131.

[6] *Manning* v. *Wasdale*, 5 A. & E. 758.

him. Subject to this condition he may dam up the stream for the purpose of a mill, or divert the water for the purpose of irrigation.[7] But he has no right to interrupt the regular flow of the stream, if he thereby interferes with the lawful use of the water by other proprietors, and inflicts upon them a sensible injury."

Source of a stream.

If the stream begins to flow in a defined channel directly it springs from the ground, these principles become at once applicable, so that the owner of the land in which it has its source cannot interrupt or appropriate it.[8]

Fouling a stream.

A riparian proprietor has further a right to have the water of a natural stream run through his land in its natural purity. In *Wood* v. *Waud*,[9] the jury found that the defendants had fouled the water of the stream by pouring in soap-suds, woolcombers' suds, &c.; but that such pollution of the natural stream had done no

No actual damage.

actual damage to the plaintiffs, because it was

[7] See *Northam* v. *Hurley*, 1 E. & B. 665, a case of grant.

[8] *Dudden* v. *Guardians of the Clutton Union*, 1 H. & N. 627; see *Ennor* v. *Barwell*, 2 Giff. 410; on appeal, 4 L. T. N. S. 597; *Brown* v. *Best*, 1 Wils. 174.

[9] 3 Exch. 748; *Stockport Water Works* v. *Potter*, 7 Jur. N. S. 880; 7 H. & N. 160; *Hipkins* v. *Birmingham, &c., Gas Company*, 5 H. & N. 74; 6 H. & N. 250.

already so polluted by similar acts of millowners above the defendants' mills, and by dyers still further up the stream, and some sewers of the town of Bradford, that the wrongful act of the defendants made no practical difference; that is, that the pollution by the defendants did not make it less applicable to useful purposes than such water was before. The Court thought, notwithstanding, that the plaintiffs had received damage in point of law. They had a right to the natural stream flowing through the land in its natural state, as an incident to the right to the land on which the watercourse flowed,[1] and that right continued except so far as it might have been derogated from by user, or by grant to the neighbouring landowners. It was a case, therefore, of an injury to a right. The defendants, by continuing the practice for twenty years, might establish the right to the easement of discharging into the stream the foul water from their works. If the dyeworks, and other manufactories and other sources of pollution above the plaintiffs, should be afterwards discontinued, the plaintiffs,

Damage in law.

[1] *Ante*, p. 123 *n* (1).

who would otherwise have had in that case pure water, would be compellable to submit to this nuisance, which then would do serious damage to them.

Injunction.

The same plaintiffs recovered a farthing damages in an action which they brought against another firm for polluting the same stream, and then applied for an injunction. This was refused on grounds which will be found stated hereafter.[1]

Weeks v. *Heward.*

In the recent case of *Weeks* v. *Heward,*[2] the defendants were polluting a stream which supplied certain watercress-beds of the plaintiff. The bill prayed in effect that they might be restrained from draining foul water, or permitting it to flow, to the spring and watercress-beds of the plaintiff, and from causing any damage or injury to such watercress-beds. An interlocutory motion for an injunction was refused, on the ground that the defendants had as much right to use the stream for drainage, as the plaintiff had for growing watercresses, in the absence of any prescriptive right.

[1] *Wood* v. *Sutcliffe*, 2 Sim. N. S. 163.
[2] 10 W. R. 557.

This case does not throw any doubt on the right of a riparian proprietor to receive the water unpolluted. If this right was asserted (which is not quite clear) the Court might well refuse to restrain a violation of it, if the only damage alleged was to an user of the water by the plaintiff which was considered to be itself excessive.

Lord Tenterden's Act. Fouling.

A claim to foul a natural stream by pouring dirty water[3] or throwing rubbish[4] into it, is within Lord Tenterden's Act.[5]

Right to water created by deed.

Rights to water may be created by deed, or parties may thereby modify the rights which they would have had as riparian proprietors.[6]

Artificial streams.

An artificial stream, produced by the drainage or other operations of one proprietor, is often not a burden merely, but also a benefit to the owner of a lower tenement through which it is conducted. The upper proprietor may gain by long

Upper and lower proprietors.

[3] *Wright* v. *Williams*, 1 M. & W. 77.

[4] *Carlyon* v. *Lovering*, 1 H. & N. 798.

[5] 2 & 3 Will. 4, c. 71; see *Murgatroyd* v. *Robinson*, 7 E. & B. 391; *Moore* v. *Webb*, 1 C. B. N. S. 673.

[6] *Northam* v. *Hurley*, 1 E. & B. 665; *Whitehead* v. *Parks*, 2 H. & N. 870; *Lee* v. *Stevenson*, 4 Jur. N. S. 950; *Wardle* v. *Brocklehurst*, 6 Jur. N. S. 374.

enjoyment a right to continue the discharge, but the lower proprietor does not so acquire a right to insist on such continuance.[7] In the absence of contract[8] an intermediate owner may, in the first instance, intercept the water, but, after twenty years' user, the lower proprietor gains a right to the flow as against him.[9] Neither the upper proprietor nor the intermediate owners may pollute the stream, as that would be throwing a greater burden upon the owners below;[1] but, of course, they may acquire a right to do so by long user.

Intermediate proprietors.

Pollution.

Distinction between natural and artificial streams.

It seems that a natural stream does not cease to be so by reason only of its flowing in an artificial bed, and on the other hand, although a stream which is created by the will or for the convenience of man, may seek out a natural channel for itself, the adjoining landowners do

[7] *Lord Falmouth* v. *Innys*, Mos. 87; *Dawson* v. *Paver*, 5 Hare, 415; *Arkwright* v. *Gell*, 5 M. & W. 203; *Greatrex* v. *Hayward*, 8 Exch. 291; *Sharp* v. *Waterhouse*, 3 Jur. N. S. 1022; *Sampson* v. *Hoddinott*, 1 C. B. N. S. 590; *Briscoe* v. *Drought*, 11 Ir. C. L. 250.

[8] *Duke of Devonshire* v. *Elgin*, 20 L. J. Ch. 495.

[9] *Wood* v. *Waud*, 3 Exch. 748; *Arkwright* v. *Gell*, 5 M. & W. 203; *Briscoe* v. *Drought*, 11 Ir. C. L. 250.

[1] *Magor* v. *Chadwick*, 11 A. & E. 571; *Wood* v. *Waud*, 3 Exch. 748.

not thereby acquire the rights of riparian proprietors.[2]

Arkwright v. Gell.

In *Arkwright* v. *Gell*,[3] a stream of water from a mineral field had flowed for more than twenty years through an artificial sough or level to the plaintiff's cotton mills. Persons in the same legal position as the owners of the field constructed another sough on a lower level so as to drain a further part of it, whereby the plaintiff's stream was diverted. It was held that no action lay for this diversion.

Wood v. Waud.

The cases were reviewed in *Wood* v. *Waud*,[4] and the rule laid down that no action will lie for an injury by the diversion of an artificial stream of water, where, from the nature of the case, it is obvious that the enjoyment of it depends upon temporary circumstances, and is not of a permanent character, and where the interruption is by a person who stands in the situation of a grantor, or (in the case of a modern stream) is a pro-

[2] *Magor* v. *Chadwick*, 11 A. & E. 571 ; *Beeston* v. *Weate*, 5 E. & B. 986 ; *North Eastern Railway Company* v. *Elliott*, 1 J. & H. 154 ; 2 D. F. & J. 423 ; *Briscoe* v. *Drought*, 11 Ir. C. L. 250 ; see *Wood* v. *Waud*, 3 Exch. 748 ; *Sampson* v. *Hoddinott*, 1 C. B. N. S. 590.

[3] 5 M. & W. 203 (decided 1839).

[4] 3 Exch. 748.

prietor and occupier of land above, through which the watercourse passes. It was thrown out, however, that possibly neither the grantors nor any other person might be at liberty to pollute the stream whilst it continued to run, apparently for the reason that this would increase the burden thrown upon the lower owner.

Magor v. Chadwick.

Again in *Magor* v. *Chadwick*,[5] it appeared that the stream claimed by the plaintiffs flowed from the mouth of an adit or underground passage, in adjoining lands not belonging to the plaintiffs, and which had been originally made more than fifty years before by the owner of a certain mine for the purpose of clearing the water from it, but that the mine had not been worked for more than thirty years past, that after the working was discontinued the plaintiffs availed themselves of the water coming along this channel to brew beer, and after clearing the adit themselves had for more than twenty years obtained from it pure water for that purpose, and had erected a brewery there at a great expense. The defendants were owners of other mines, and

[5] 11 Ad. & El. 571 (decided 1840).

had lately used the old adit for the purpose of draining them, and had thereby fouled the water, and made it unfit for brewing. It was not shown that they were connected with or claimed under the owners of the adit or of the first mine or of the lands through which the water flowed.

The defendants contended that a custom prevailed in Cornwall, by virtue of which an adit once made might at any time be again employed for that purpose. The jury negatived the custom. The learned judge (Patteson, J.) directed the jury that in the absence of custom artificial water-courses[6] are not distinguishable in law from such as are natural, and that twenty years' enjoyment would therefore warrant the jury in finding in favour of the right. A rule *nisi* for a new trial on the ground of misdirection was discharged, Lord Denman saying that the custom was not expressly pleaded, and that the defendants were not the makers of the adit, but were strangers and wrong-doers. It was suggested that those who formed the channel might have a superior right to the plaintiffs.

[6] Meaning apparently artificial channels, and not, as it has been sometimes taken, streams artificially produced.

CHAP. II. Sect. 3

Greatrex v. Hayward.

So in *Greatrex* v. *Hayward*,[7] it was held that the flow of water for twenty years from a drain made for the purpose of agricultural improvements, does not give a right to the neighbour so as to preclude the proprietor from altering the level of his drain.

Whalley v. Laing

In *Whalley* v. *Laing*,[8] the plaintiffs made a cut from a canal, by the permission of the owners, and conducted water through it to their own premises. Afterwards the defendants discharged foul water into the canal from their works, the owners of the canal not forbidding it, whereby the water which the plaintiffs drew off became less fit for use. It was held that the action could not be maintained on the pleadings as they stood, and it was the opinion of some of the learned judges that the facts disclosed no cause of action.

Definition of a watercourse.

A watercourse is said[9] to be "a flow of water possessing that unity of character by which the flow on one person's land can be identified with

[7] 8 Exch. 291 (decided 1853).

[8] 2 H. & N. 476; 3 H. & N. 675, 901.

[9] *Briscoe* v. *Drought*, 11 Ir. C. L. 250; per Christian, J.

that on his neighbour's." Such a flow will generally, and perhaps necessarily, take place in a defined channel either above or below ground.[1] We have now to deal with water which does not flow in this manner, but is either diffused over the surface or percolates underground.

Water not flowing in a defined channel.

Drainage.

The owner of land lying on a lower level is bound to receive the water which drains naturally from land on a higher level; but the upper proprietor, by a particular system of drainage or otherwise, may cause such water to flow on to his neighbour's premises in an injurious manner so as to give a cause of action.[2]

Property in water.

The general law respecting the right to streams is not applicable to water which does not flow in any defined channel. Any landowner may collect and appropriate as much of such water as he pleases, either from the surface or by digging a well,[3] or he may drain it away for the better culti-

[1] *Dickenson* v. *Grand Junction Canal Company*, 7 Exch. 300; *Chasemore* v. *Richards*, 7 H. L. C. 349; *Rex* v. *Inhabitants of Oxfordshire*, 1 B. & Ad. 301.

[2] *Haward* v. *Bankes*, 2 Burr. 1113; *Smith* v. *Kenrick*, 7 C. B. 515; 18 L. J. C. P. 172.

[3] *Hammond* v. *Hall*, 10 Sim. 551; *Chasemore* v. *Richards*, 7 H. L. C. 349; *New River Company* v. *Johnson*, 6 Jur. N. S. 374.

CHAP. II. Sect. 3.

vation of his lands,[4] or in the course of mining or other works,[5] notwithstanding that the effect may be to leave his neighbour's land dry.

Water in mines.

Although, as a general rule, a man is bound not to allow his drainage water to flow on to his neighbour's land injuriously, yet the owner of a coal mine who works it in an ordinary and proper manner[6] is not responsible for a flow of water which may thus be occasioned into a neighbouring mine,[7] the miner's maxim being that water is a common enemy, against which every man must protect himself.

Barriers.

The practice is said to be that each owner works to the end of his boundary on the dip of his beds, and leaves a barrier of his own mineral on the rise.[8] If an upper owner trespasses upon the barrier of a lower owner he is liable for the conse-

[4] *Balston* v. *Bensted*, 1 Camp. 463 (overruled); *Rawstron* v. *Taylor*, 11 Exch. 369; *Broadbent* v. *Ramsbotham*, 11 Exch. 602. As to public drainage, see *Manchester, &c., Company* v. *Worksop Board of Health*, 23 Beav. 198; *Stainton* v. *Woolrych*, 23 Beav. 225.

[5] *Acton* v. *Blundell*, 12 M. & W. 324; *Galgay* v. *G. S. and W. Railway*, 4 Ir. C. L. 456.

[6] *Walker* v. *Fletcher*, 3 Bli. 172.

[7] *Firmstone* v. *Wheeley*, 2 Dowl. & L. 203; *Smith* v. *Kenrick*, 7 C. B. 515; 18 L. J. C. P. 172; *Duke of Beaufort* v. *Morris*, 6 Ha. 346; 2 Phil. 683.

[8] Bainbridge on Mines, 426.

quential damage as well as for the value of the coal, but he is not bound to fill up the excavation which he has made.[9] But in *Lord Mexborough* v. *Bower*,[1] the tenant of a colliery was restrained by his landlord from allowing a communication, which the tenant had opened with an adjoining mine in breach of covenant, to remain open.

Drowned mine.

The existence of water in a drowned mine may produce an indirect benefit to the adjacent tenements. But as such a state of things is obviously accidental and temporary, no right can be acquired by prescription to resist the withdrawal of the water.[2]

Flood water.

Altering the ancient course of flood water so as to throw it in greater quantity upon a neighbour's land, appears to be a nuisance of a similar kind to diverting a stream flowing in a bounded channel.[3]

[9] *Clegg* v. *Dearden*, 12 Q. B. 576; *Powell* v. *Aiken*, 4 K. & J. 343.

[1] 7 Beav. 127.

[2] *Birmingham Canal Company* v. *Lloyd*, 18 Ves. 516; *North Eastern Railway Company* v. *Elliott*, 1 J. & H. 145; 2 D. F. & J. 423, now in H. L.

[3] *Rex* v. *Trafford*, 1 B. & Ad. 874; *Trafford* v. *Rex* (in error), 1 M. & Sc. 401; 8 Bing. 204; 2 C. & J. 265; 2 Tyr. 201; see *Wicks* v. *Hunt*, J. 372; *Lawrence* v. *Great Northern Railway Company*, 16 Q. B. 643.

CHAP. II. Sect. 3. Injunctions.

Substantial damage.

Injunctions of course lie to protect the legal rights of riparian proprietors to the flow[4] or purity[5] of a stream, but substantial damage must be shown to exist either in the way of loss of enjoyment of the stream,[6] or, as in *The Rochdale Canal Company* v. *King*,[7] by loss of the profit which the plaintiffs could have obtained by licensing the infringement. There the Rochdale Canal Company was a company established for the purpose of making and maintaining a canal, which the public had a right to use on the payment of tolls. Special privileges were given to particular persons of drawing off a certain quan-

Rochdale Canal Company v. King.

[4] Cary, 36; *Finch* v. *Resbridge*, 2 Vern. 390; *Bush* v. *Western*, Prec. Ch. 530; *Weller* v. *Smeaton*, 1 Bro. C. C. 572; *Robinson* v. *Lord Byron*, 1 Bro. C. C. 588; 2 Cox, 4; *Kerrison* v. *Sparrow*, 19 Ves. 449; G. Coop. 305; *Dewhirst* v. *Wrigley*, 1 C. P. Coop. 319; *Elwell* v. *Crowther*, 10 W. R. 615; 6 L. T. N. S. 596.

[5] *Elmhirst* v. *Spencer*, 2 Mac. & Gor. 45; *Wood* v. *Sutcliffe*, 2 Sim. N. S. 163; *Oldaker* v. *Hunt*, 6 D. M. & G. 376; 3 Eq. Rep. 671; *Attorney General* v. *Luton Board of Health*, 2 Jur. N. S. 180; *Manchester, Sheffield, and Lincoln Railway Company* v. *Worksop Board of Health*, 23 Beav. 198; *Attorney-General* v. *Borough of Birmingham*, 4 K. & J. 528; Seton on Decrees, 3rd ed. 894.

[6] *Elmhirst* v. *Spencer*, 2 Mac. & Gor. 45; *Wood* v. *Sutcliffe*, 2 Sim. N. S. 163; *Attorney-General* v. *Manchester and Leeds Railway Company*, 1 Rlwy. Ca. 436,

[7] 2 Sim. N. S. 78; 14 Q. B. 122; 16 Beav. 630; *Rochdale Canal Company* v. *Radcliffe*, 21 L. J. Q. B. 297; see *Tipping* v. *Eckersley*, 2 K. & J. 264.

tity of water for particular purposes, and the surplus was given to the Duke of Bridgewater. The company obtained a shilling damages from a mill-owner on the bank, who was drawing off water for an unauthorised purpose, but not so as to obstruct the navigation. They then applied for an injunction, which was resisted on the ground that the subject matter was too trifling for the interference of a Court of Equity. Lord Cranworth, V.-C., dissented from that proposition, saying that if the title of the plaintiffs was once clearly established, the right was one of great value, though the damages recovered in each particular action might be very small or merely nominal; for the necessities of the defendants would oblige them to pay a water-rent for the right required.

Wood v. Sutcliffe.

The principles upon which injunctions of this kind depend are fully considered in the case of *Wood* v. *Sutcliffe*.[6] The facts were that the plaintiffs had acquired by long enjoyment the right of using the water of the stream for washing wool and generating and condensing

[6] 2 Sim. N. S. 163 ; *Wood* v. *Waud*, 3 Exch. 748.

steam. The defendants, who were dyers, had poured the refuse of the matters used in their business into a drain, communicating with the stream, and so polluted it, for which the plaintiffs brought an action against them, and recovered a farthing damages. Afterwards a bill was filed, and upon a motion for an injunction, Kindersley, V.-C., said: "I conceive that if parties have established such a legal right as the plaintiffs in this case have established, and another person comes and erects works on the same stream, above their works, and, by his manufacturing process, so fouls the water of the stream as seriously and continuously to obstruct the effective carrying on of their manufacture; and, if the granting of an injunction will restore, or tend to restore those parties to the position in which they previously stood, and in which they have a right to stand; and if the injury complained of is of such a nature that damages will not be an adequate compensation, that is, such a compensation as will in effect, though not in specie, place them in the position in which they previously stood; and if, moreover (for there are several conditions), they use due diligence in

Farthing damages.

Legal right.

Restoring position.

Damages not an adequate compensation.

Duo diligenc

vindicating their rights, they have, in general, a right to come to a Court of Equity and say: 'Do not leave us to bring action after action for the purpose of recovering damages, but interfere, with a strong hand, and prevent the continuance of the acts we complain of, in order that our legal right may be protected and preserved to us.' I say, in general; because, whenever a Court of Equity is asked for an injunction in cases of such a nature as this, it must have regard not only to the dry, strict rights of the plaintiff and defendant, but also to the surrounding circumstances; to the rights or interests of other persons which may be more or less involved: it must, I say, have regard to those circumstances before it exercises its jurisdiction (which is unquestionably a strong one) of granting an injunction. I have used the terms 'seriously obstruct,' because I cannot assent to the proposition that, on the mere dry fact of the plaintiffs having the abstract right, a Court of Equity will, as a matter of course, on that right being established at law, grant an injunction if the right be infringed ever so minutely. On the other hand, I am far from saying that because, in the action at law, the jury has given only a

Rights or interests of other persons.

Nature of obstruction.

CHAP. II. Sect. 3.

shilling, or a farthing damages, *that* is a ground for concluding that the injury is not serious, and that the case is one in which an injunction ought not to be granted. I have used, also, the terms 'continuously obstruct,' by which I mean to indicate 'obstruction frequently recurring,' not 'never ceasing.'

"Having stated the conditions which are requisite to induce the Court to grant an injunction in such a case, I proceed to consider how far those conditions are satisfied in the present case. One of those conditions is that the injunction, by stopping the acts complained of, will restore or tend to restore the party complaining, to the enjoyment of that right which he has established against the defendant. I say 'restore or tend to restore,' because I conceive it is no answer to an application of this sort, for the defendant to say that other persons, as well as he, are polluting the stream, and that therefore the injunction will not restore the plaintiff to the enjoyment of his legal right, inasmuch as it will not prevent those other persons from continuing to pollute the water; for the plaintiff must sue each of the wrong-doers separately; unless,

Others polluting the stream.

indeed, they are acting in partnership or in concert together; and the obtaining of an injunction against any one of the wrong-doers, though it may not actually restore, does tend to restore the plaintiff to the enjoyment of his right, as it is a step towards obtaining an injunction against each of them.

"Now the plaintiffs require water for three purposes; namely, washing wool, generating steam, and condensing steam; for the first two of which, purity is an essential quality. Not only the defendants, but the Messrs. Ripley, and other persons, have manufactories on the banks of the stream, above the plaintiffs' mills. The works of Messrs. Ripley, who are dyers, were established long before the plaintiffs' mills were; but the works of the other persons were established at a comparatively recent period. Besides those various works, a very large and dense population has gradually grown up on or near to the banks of the stream. No doubt, however, there was a time, and probably not a very remote one, when the stream, or that portion of it which lies between Messrs. Ripley's works and the plaintiffs' mills, flowed through open fields, pure

Pollution inevitable by reason of the population.

and unpolluted, to the plaintiffs' mills. But whenever human beings congregate in large numbers on the banks of a stream, the inevitable consequence is, that a great quantity of sewerage is discharged into the stream, which necessarily has the effect of polluting it. Therefore, to some considerable extent, the pollution of this stream is inevitable. Not all the courts of law and equity in the kingdom can prevent it; for they cannot remove the mass of human beings who are congregated on the banks of the stream. The plaintiffs themselves have been obliged to submit to the inevitable consequence of this increase of population, and have been compelled to procure pure water from another source, by sinking a well on their own premises for that purpose; and for many years before the defendants commenced their works, the plaintiffs ceased to use the water of the stream for washing wool, and used it only occasionally, that is to say, when the machinery of the well was out of order, even for the purpose of generating steam. Therefore, if this injunction were granted, it would not have the effect of restoring, or tending to restore, the plaintiffs to the position in which they originally stood; for the water would still flow to their mills in so polluted a state that they could not use it, as they originally did, for either washing wool or generating steam.

Injunction a great injury to the defendants.

"On the other hand, to grant the injunction would have the effect of seriously injuring, if not ruining the defendants. Weighing, then, the injury that may accrue, to the one party or the other, by granting or refusing the injunction, I think that, if my decision were to turn upon this point alone, I should be bound to refuse it.

Damages an adequate compensation.

"Another condition which, as I have said, is necessary in order to induce a Court of Equity to interfere, by injunction, in a case similar to that now before me, is that the mischief complained of is such that it cannot be properly and adequately compensated by pecuniary damages.

"Now let us see how the matter stands in this respect. Many years before the defendants' works were commenced, Mr. Dixon, Messrs. Greenwood, and other individuals, had works in what is, aptly enough, called the nest of factories immediately above the plaintiffs' mills; and they, also, having polluted the stream, the plaintiffs threatened to bring actions against them: whereupon they entered into deeds of arrangement with the plaintiffs, by which, in order to avoid litigation, they agreed to pay the plaintiffs at the rate of 2*l.* per annum per horse-power, for the right of polluting the water. Now, if such an arrangement as that can be made, ought I to grant an injunction in order to compel the defendants to enter into it, when the bringing of an action would be almost (I will not say quite) as efficacious? If the plaintiffs desire to apply to the defendants a certain pressure, in order to bring them to terms, I think that I ought to leave plaintiffs to that pressure which may be applied by means of an action or actions at law. If the plaintiffs brought an action, and, the matter being represented to the jury, the jury were satisfied that the defendants ought to come to terms, they might give the plaintiffs 50*l.* or 100*l.* damages, instead of a farthing, a shilling, or forty shillings. On the ground, therefore, that the plaintiffs themselves have shown that the injury they complain of is one which, in some way, may be compensated by money, I think that I ought not to grant the injunction.

Ground of decision.

"But I do not rest my decision upon either of the grounds which I have mentioned. The principal ground upon which I conceive that I must refuse this injunction, is that the plaintiffs have not used due diligence in vindicating their rights. They stood by whilst the defendants were constructing their works, and they suffered the defendants to use their works after they were constructed, from the beginning of 1845, until the beginning of 1850, a period of nearly five years, without giving them any hint that they were doing anything that they had not a lawful right to do; and if there had been nothing else in this case, I should have been of opinion, on this ground alone, that the plaintiffs were not entitled to the injunction.

Want of due diligence.

Other grounds.

"I incline to think also that the injunction ought to be refused on the ground that the injury complained of is capable of being compensated in money; and in my opinion it ought also to be refused on the ground that the granting of it would inflict serious damage on the defendant without doing any real practical good to the plaintiffs."

Repairing watercourse.

In *M'Swiney* v. *Haynes*,[2] the plaintiff was the proprietor of extensive mills, which he had enjoyed, together with the mill-stream and the waters incident thereto, for upwards of twenty years. An ancient weir extended across the river from the mouth of the plaintiff's mill-race to the defendant's grounds on the other side of the stream, and turned into the mill-race the whole of the stream when necessary. The plaintiff was accustomed to repair the weir. The defendant having ploughed near to the bank on his side, a heavy flood burst through, making an entirely new passage for the stream, and leaving the plaintiff's mill-race dry. The plaintiff claimed to go on to the defendant's land, in order to make the necessary repairs, and the defendant was restrained on an *ex parte* motion from preventing him from so doing.

[2] 1 Ir. Eq. 322; *Peter* v. *Daniel*, 5 C. B. 568.

Sect. 4.—NUISANCES RELATING TO SUPPORT.

Sect. 4.

Soil. Lateral support.

The Common Law gives to every land-owner the right to have his own soil in its natural state supported by the adjoining soil or by some equivalent, so that no one is entitled to remove his own soil in such a manner as to cause his neighbour's land in its natural state to fall in.[3]

Soil. Vertical support.

In mining districts, the surface and the strata lying under it frequently belong to different persons. Originally there must have been unity of title, either in the Crown or a subject, from the surface to the centre of the earth, and the mutual rights will generally have been ascertained and settled at the time of the severance. But where the soil lying over the minerals belongs to one man, and the minerals to another, no evidence of title appearing to regulate or qualify the enjoyment, the owner of the surface unincumbered by

3 *Wilde* v. *Minsterley*, 2 Roll. Abr. 564 ; *Wyatt* v. *Harrison*, 3 B. & Ad. 871 ; *Hunt* v. *Peake*, J. 705 ; *North Eastern Railway Company* v. *Elliott*, 1 J. & H. 154 ; 2 D. F. & J. 423 ; now on appeal to the House of Lords.

Chap. II. Sect. 4.

buildings, and in its natural state, is entitled to have it supported from below.[4]

Excavated soil.

A man may so weaken his soil by mining or other excavations under it, that the surface shall require more lateral support than before. It is not settled whether there is a natural right to such additional support, but if not it may probably be gained by long enjoyment.[5]

Modern buildings.

These rights of lateral and vertical support extend to buildings not so heavy as sensibly to increase the tendency of the soil to subside.[6] But there is no right of support from the adjacent land for new buildings which exceed that weight.[7]

[4] *Lewis* v. *Marsh*, 8 Hare, 97; *Humphries* v. *Brogden*, 12 Q. B. 739; *Smart* v. *Morton*, 5 E. & B. 30; *Rowbotham* v. *Wilson*, 6 E. & B. 593; 8 E. & B. 123; 8 H. L. C. 348; *Roberts* v. *Haines*, 6 E. & B. 643; 7 E. & B. 625.

[5] *Partridge* v. *Scott*, 3 M. & W. 220; *Browne* v. *Robins*, 4 H. & N. 186; see *post*, Ancient Buildings.

[6] *Smart* v. *Morton*, 5 E. & B. 30; *Roberts* v. *Haines*, 6 E. & B. 643; 7 E. & B. 625; *Bonomi* v. *Backhouse*, E. B. & E. 622; 9 W. R. 769; *Brown* v. *Robins*, 4 H. & N. 186; *Hunt* v. *Peake*, J. 705; *Stroyan* v. *Knowles*, 6 H. & N. 454. See as to letting down the bed of a watercourse, *Elwell* v. *Crowther*, 10 W. R. 615; 6 L. T. N. S. 596.

[7] *Wilde* v. *Minsterley*, 2 Roll. Abr. 564; *Palmer* v. *Fletcher*, 1 Sid. 167, 222; *Wyatt* v. *Harrison*, 3 B. & Ad. 871; *Dodd* v. *Holme*, 1 A. & E. 493; *Partridge* v. *Scott*, 3 M. & W. 220; *Gayford* v. *Nicholls*, 9 Exch. 702; *Caledonian Railway Company* v. *Sprot*, 2 Macq. 449; *North Eastern Railway Company* v. *Elliott*, 1 J. & H. 154; 2 D. F. & J. 423; now on appeal to the House of Lords.

It has been intimated, however, that there may be such a right of vertical support.[8]

Ancient buildings. Lateral support from soil.

There are many and clear dicta to the effect that a right to lateral support for heavy buildings from the adjacent soil may be acquired by twenty years' enjoyment.[9] These dicta are not easy to reconcile with principle. The right appears to be a negative easement, and therefore not within Lord Tenterden's Act,[1] and it is going very far to say that the forbearance of the neighbour in not digging along the boundary of his land so as to let the house down, is a sufficient reason for presuming a grant or covenant not to do so.[2]

Ancient buildings. Vertical support.

The same considerations apply with equal or greater force to vertical support. There is very little authority as to this.[3]

[8] *Rogers* v. *Taylor*, 2 H. & N. 828.

[9] *Wilde* v. *Minsterley*, 2 Roll. Abr. 564; *Palmer* v. *Fletcher*, 1 Sid. 167, 222; *Stansell* v. *Jollard*, 1 Sel. N. P. 11th edit. 457; *Wyatt* v. *Harrison*, 3 B. & Ad. 871; *Dodd* v. *Holme*, 1 A. & E. 493; *Partridge* v. *Scott*, 3 M. & W. 220; *Hide* v. *Thornborough*, 2 C. & K. 250; *Humphries* v. *Brogden*, 12 Q. B. 739; *Gayford* v. *Nicholls*, 9 Exch. 702; *Rowbotham* v. *Wilson*, 6 E. & B. 593; 8 E. & B. 123; 8 H. L. C. 348; *Bonomi* v. *Backhouse*, E. B. & E. 622; 9 W. R. 769; see *Brown* v. *Robins*, 4 H. & N. 186; *Solomon* v. *Vintners' Company*, 4 H. & N. 583; *Hunt* v. *Peake*, J. 710.

[1] *Harbidge* v. *Warwick*, 3 Exch. 557.

[2] *Webb* v. *Bird*, 10 C. B. N. S. 268; in error, 8 Jur. N. S. 621.

[3] *Rowbotham* v. *Wilson*, 6 E. & B. 593; 8 E. & B. 123; 8 H. L. C. 348; *Rogers* v. *Taylor*, 2 H. & N. 828.

CHAP. II.
Sect. 4.
Right of support by severance.

It is of importance to bear in mind that even if the buildings or other works are modern, yet if the land on which they are placed, and the subjacent or adjacent strata can be shown to have belonged to the same person, a right of support, in excess of the ordinary common law right, may, and frequently will, have arisen from the manner of the severance.[4] This is explained in the *Caledonian Railway Company* v. *Sprot*,[5] where it is said, "If the owner of a house were to convey the upper story to a purchaser, reserving all below the upper story, such purchaser would, on general principles, have a right to prevent the owner of the lower stories from interfering with the walls and beams upon which the upper story rests, so as to prevent them from affording proper support. The same principle applies to the case of adjacent support, so far, at all events, as to prevent a person who has granted part of his land from so dealing with that which he retains, as to cause that which he has granted to sink or fall.

Caledonian Railway Company v. Sprot.

[4] *Rogers* v. *Taylor*, 2 H. & N. 828.

[5] 2 Macq. 449; see *Bush* v. *Field*, Cary, 128; *Harris* v. *Ryding*, 5 M. & W. 60; *Smart* v. *Morton*, 5 E. & B. 30; *Rowbotham* v. *Wilson*, 6 E. & B. 593; 8 E. & B. 123; 8 H. L. C. 348; *North Eastern Railway Company* v. *Elliott*, 1 J. & H. 154; 2 D. F. & J. 423; now on appeal to the House of Lords.

Extent of support for land granted.

"How far such adjacent support must extend is a question which in each particular case will depend on its own special circumstances. If the line dividing that which is granted from that which is retained traverses a quarry of hard stone or marble, it may be that no adjacent support at all is necessary. If, on the other hand, it traverses a bed of sand, or a marsh, or a loose gravelly soil, it may be that a considerable breadth of support is necessary to prevent the land granted from falling away upon the soil of what is retained. Again, if the surface of the land granted is merely a common meadow or a ploughed field, the necessity for support will probably be much less than if it were covered with buildings or trees. And it must further be observed, that all which a grantor can reasonably be considered to grant or warrant is such a measure of support, subjacent or adjacent, as is necessary for the land in its condition at the time of the grant, or in the state for the purpose of putting it into which the grant is made.[6] Thus, if I grant a meadow to another, retaining both

[6] *Harris v. Ryding*, 5 M. & W. 63.

the minerals under it, and also the adjoining lands, I am bound so to work my mines, and to dig my adjoining lands as not to cause the meadow to sink to or fall over. But if I do this, and the grantee thinks fit to build a house on the edge of the land he has acquired, he cannot complain of my workings or diggings, if by reason of the additional weight he has put on the land they cause his house to fall. If, indeed, the grant is made expressly to enable the grantee to build his house on the land granted, then there is an implied warranty of support, subjacent and adjacent, as if the house already existed."[7]

Extent of support for land retained.

We have seen that the grantor is presumed to grant such support as is necessary for the land granted in its condition at the time, or in the state for the purpose of putting it into which the grant is made. The measure of the support which he is presumed to retain appears in general to be only that which is necessary for the land retained in its condition at the time of the severance.[8]

[7] See *Caledonian Railway Company* v. *Belhaven*, 3 Macq. 56.
[8] *Dugdale* v. *Robertson*, 3 K. & J. 700 ; *Pinnington* v. *Galland*, 9 Exch. 1.

Working minerals near to and under a railway or canal.

In Acts of Parliament authorising the construction of canals or railways over a mineral district, provisions are commonly inserted enabling the company to postpone the purchase of the minerals until such times as the colliery owners may wish to work them. One of the earliest cases which arose on clauses of this nature was *Wyrley Canal Navigation* v. *Bradley*.[9] Sect. 6 of the Canal Act provided that the company should not be entitled on purchasing lands, to any coal mines, &c., under the same, but that such mines should belong to the same persons as would have been entitled to them if the Act had not passed; and sect. 61 enacted that when the owner of any mine should be desirous of working the same within ten yards of the canal, he should give notice to the company, who might thereupon stop the proposed working and make compensation, or otherwise the owner was thereby authorised to work such part of the mine as lay under the canal, or within the distance aforesaid.

Wyrley Canal v. Bradley.

Power to purchase the minerals.

It appeared in evidence that the defendants gave notice of their intention to work within the

[9] 7 East, 368.

specified distance, and the company declined to purchase. The defendants thereupon continued working the mine *in the usual way*, till damage happened by the partial giving way of the sides and bottom of the canal. Upon these facts the learned judge nonsuited the plaintiffs, and upon a motion to set the nonsuit aside, "All the court were of opinion that the meaning of the Act of Parliament in requiring the coal-owners to give notice of their intention to work the mines within a certain distance of the canal, and the liberty given to the company to inspect the works and prohibit the owners, upon making compensation to them, for working within that distance, was for the purpose of enabling the company to purchase out the rights of the coal-owners if they thought their canal works likely to be endangered by the nearer approach of the miners, but if the company declined the purchase, as they had done in this case, the coal-owners were left to their common law rights, as if no canal had been made, and they might take every part of their coal in the same manner as they might have done before the Act passed; their former rights in that respect not having been taken away by the Act, which had only appropriated the surface of the land and so much of the soil as was necessary for the cutting and making of the canal, leaving the coal, &c., to the owners, to be enjoyed in the same manner as before; and the legislature had only given the land-owners a compensation for so much of the soil as they had deprived them of. And this they said was not like the case where damages were recovered against the late Earl of Lonsdale for undermining a person's house, for there the party claimed under a grant from the owner of the land, and the injury done was against the land-owner's own grant."

Power to purchase and no injury to be done to the navigation.

Dudley Canal *v.* Grazebrook.

The Act in the *Dudley Canal Navigation Company* v. *Grazebrook*,[1] contained similar provisions as to notice and purchase; but by the clause reserving the rights of mine-owners, it was enacted that subject to the conditions and restrictions in the Act contained, it should be lawful for the owners to work their mines "*provided no injury be done to the said navigation.*" The company having declined to purchase the subjacent

[1] 1 B. & Ad. 59; *Birmingham Canal Company* v. *Hawkesford*, 7 East, 371; see *Cromford Canal* v. *Cutts*, 5 Rlwy. Ca. 442; *Barnsley Canal* v. *Twibell*, 13 L. J. Ch. 434.

minerals after due notice, the defendants proceeded to work them *in the ordinary and usual mode*, and damage ensued to the canal.

The Court said that the only doubt that the defendants were justified in doing what they had done arose upon the proviso before mentioned. That it could not mean that the owners were to be responsible at all events for any injury or damage done to the canal, for then the company would never purchase the minerals. That the reasonable mode of reconciling the different parts of the Act was to say "either that the party working the mines is to do no unnecessary damage or injury to the navigation, or no extraordinary damage or injury by working them out of the ordinary and usual mode."

Compensation.

Of course in cases like the above, the company in the first instance do not give compensation for the minerals lying within the specified distance. But where[2] no liberty was given to the company to purchase upon notice, but it was enacted that mines might be worked by the owner, so that no damage should thereby be done to the

[2] *Rex* v. *Leeds and Selby Railway Company*, 3 A. & E. 683.

railway, and in case any damage should occur it was to be repaired by the owners, or at their expense, a different rule was laid down. The owner of the land, and the minerals under it, sold the surface to the company, no compensation being made for the minerals, or any present or future effect the railroad might have in regard to them. It was subsequently found that in order to get the minerals without letting down the railroad it was necessary to work in an unusually expensive way, and the owner thereupon claimed compensation. It was held that he came too late, for the claim ought to have been brought forward when the land was sold.

Railway Clauses Consolidation Act.

By the Railway Clauses Consolidation Act[3] it is enacted with respect to mines lying under or near a railway to the following effect.

Sect. 77. The Company shall not be entitled to any mines under any lands purchased by them (except such part as may be required for the construction of the works), unless the same shall have been expressly purchased, and all such

[3] 8 & 9 Vict. c. 20.

mines shall be deemed to be excepted out of the conveyance, unless they shall have been expressly named therein.

Sect. 78. If the owner of any mines or minerals lying under the railway, or within forty yards therefrom, shall be desirous of working the same, he shall give thirty days' notice to the company, whereupon the company may cause the mines to be inspected, and if it shall appear that the working of such mines and minerals is likely to damage the works of the railway, and the company is willing to make compensation to the owner, he shall not work or get the same.

Sect. 79. If before the expiration of thirty days the company do not state their willingness to treat with such owner, it shall be lawful for him to work the said mines, or any part thereof for which the company shall not have agreed to pay compensation, "so that the same be done in a manner proper and necessary for the beneficial working thereof, and according to the usual manner of working such mines in the district where the same shall be situate." And if any damage is done to the railway by improper working, it is to be repaired at the expense of the owner.

This last clause appears to ratify the rule laid down in the authorities above cited, that, if the company is unwilling to give compensation for the minerals lying within the prescribed distance, the owner may work them in a reasonable way, without regard to any damage which may result to the railway.

Common law right of support.

We next come to a very important case which turned upon the common law right of the company to support independently of any statute.

Caledonian Railway Company v. Sprot.

In the *Caledonian Railway Company* v. *Sprot*,[4] the defendant sold the land to the company by private arrangement, and conveyed it (reserving the mines) by a deed in Scotch form.[5] By the 11th section of the company's original Act it was enacted, that owners might receive satisfaction for the value of their lands, and for damages to be sustained by making and completing the works in gross sums, that any proprietor might reserve the minerals out of his

[4] 2 Macq. 449.

[5] It is not stated whether this deed had any special statutory effect. See 5 H. & N. 692.

Chap. II. Sect. 4.

bargain and sale to the company, but that it should not be lawful for him to work them without giving good security to the company for all damages which might thereby ensue. Lord Cranworth, in advising the House of Lords, said, "The first observation which occurs on this section is, that though under its provisions and other clauses of the Act, Mr. Sprot might have been compelled to sell the land in question to the company; yet when by arrangement between him and the company, it was settled what should be the price paid, and the conveyance is made accordingly; the effect of the transaction, so far as relates to the conveyance of the land and the rights acquired under it, must depend on the terms of the deed, subject only to the provision in the clause regulating or restricting the right of working the mines.

"By virtue of the conveyance the company acquired, by grant from Mr. Sprot, an absolute right to the surface of the land, and, by implication, a further right to such subjacent and adjacent support as was necessary, taking into account the purpose to which the land was to be put. Mr. Sprot, on the other hand, retained his former right of working the mines, subject to the rights which he had impliedly granted of subjacent and adjacent support, and subject also to the statutory restriction in the 11th clause, preventing him from working the mines under the land conveyed, without first giving to the company good and sufficient security for all damage which might accrue to it from such working."

This case establishes the important rule, that a company have the same right of support as an ordinary grantee, except so far as that right may be qualified by statutory provisions. It will have been observed that the Act did not contain any clause giving the company an option to purchase subjacent minerals when they were about to be got. The principle of the earlier cases, as we have seen, was that when the company had this option as to minerals lying within a specified distance, it was a strong circumstance to show that if they refused to purchase, the risk of working such minerals in the usual way was to be borne by them; and this principle has apparently not been shaken. Thus, where a company, constituted under the Lands Clauses and Railway

Fletcher *v.* Great Western Railway Company.

Clauses Consolidation Acts, had purchased by agreement from owners in fee, and it was contended on their behalf, that the grantors were not entitled to work the minerals lying under and within forty yards of the railway, in any manner likely to endanger it, although the company were unwilling to purchase, the argument did not prevail, because the 78th clause of the Railway Clauses Consolidation Acts varies the common law rights of the parties to the conveyance with respect to operations within the specified distance.

Private assurance.

It was suggested in this case[6] that there might be a distinction between cases where the conveyance to the company was an ordinary private assurance, and where it was made under the powers of the Lands Clauses Consolidation Act; but nothing seems to turn upon this.[7]

North Eastern Railway Company v. Elliott.

We have next the case of the *North Eastern Railway Company* v. *Elliott*.[8] There the Durham

[6] *Fletcher* v. *Great Western Railway Company*, 4 H. & N. 242; 5 H. & N. 689; *Swindills* v. *Birmingham Canal Navigation*, 9 C. B. N. S. 241.

[7] *North Eastern Railway Company* v. *Elliott*, 2 D. F. & J. 423; but see *Wyrley Canal Company* v. *Bradley*, 7 East, 368.

[8] 1 J. & H. 145; 2 D. F. & J. 423; now on appeal to the House of Lords.

Junction Act, 1834, enacted, by section 27, that nothing in the Act contained should extend to give the company any coal under any lands purchased, but that all such coal should be deemed to be excepted out of the purchase of such lands, and might be worked by the owner, as if the Act had not passed, "so that no damage or obstruction be done or thereby occur, to or in such railway, or other works." And by section 28, it was enacted that when the person working should approach within twenty yards of any masonry or building belonging to the company, he should give notice, and the company might then declare an election to purchase; and in default, the owner might work the minerals, "provided the same be worked in the usual and ordinary manner of working mines, and that no avoidable damage be done to the said masonry and buildings." Sect. 27 seems to express the ordinary right of a grantee at common law, and sect. 28 received a construction similar to that placed upon sect. 78 of the Railway Clauses Consolidation Act.

The defendant was restrained from working within the twenty yards until he should have

CHAP. II. Sect. 4.

given notice to the company, pursuant to the 28th sect.; and from working at any time beyond the twenty yards in such a manner as to affect the stability of the railway.

Stourbridge Canal Company v. Earl Dudley.

Again, in the *Stourbridge Canal Company* v. *Earl Dudley*,[9] the Act (16 Geo. 3, c. 28), provided, that if an owner wished to work any mines within twelve yards of the canal, he was to give notice, and the company might then purchase, or otherwise the owner might work such mines provided "no injury be done to the said navigation." The company having omitted to purchase after notice, the mines were worked within the twelve yards, in the *usual and ordinary mode;* but, nevertheless, damage was done to the navigation. It was held, on the authority of the *Dudley Canal Company* v. *Grazebrook*, that the company were not entitled to recover against the owner.

Reg. v. Aire and Calder Navigation.

On the other hand, in *Reg.* v. *Aire and Calder Navigation*,[1] the owners had power to get the minerals, doing no injury to the canal, but there were no clauses giving the company an option to

[9] 30 L. J. Q. B. 108.
[1] 30 L. J. Q. B. 337.

purchase any of the minerals. It was known at the time of the conveyance that there were coals under the lands conveyed, and the purchase money was agreed upon and paid with that knowledge. The company, under the powers of their Act, prevented the working of certain beds of coal, on the ground that it would be injurious to the canal. It was held, following *Rex* v. *Leeds and Selby Railway Company*, that the owner had no right to further compensation.

London and North Western Railway Company v. Ackroyd.

Lastly, in *The London and North Western Railway Company* v. *Ackroyd*,[2] an owner in fee granted to the company the right of making and for ever maintaining and using a tunnel. The company endeavoured to establish a right to support from minerals lying within forty yards, without making compensation, under the 78th sect. of the Railway Clauses Consolidation Act. Wood, V.-C., was of opinion that the case was entirely within the authority of *Fletcher* v. *Great Western Railway Company*, and that the contention of the company had therefore failed.

Tunnel.

[2] 10 W. R. 367.

CHAP. II. Sect. 4.

Result of the authorities.

The result, therefore, seems to be, that as to minerals lying beyond the specified distance, the company have an absolute right of support; but that as to minerals lying within the specified distance, if the company have power to purchase and omit to do so after due notice, the owner may work such minerals in the usual way, without being answerable for any subsidence which may take place.

Compensation.

The 81st section of the Railway Clauses Consolidation Act[3] enacts, that the company shall from time to time make compensation for any minerals not purchased by the company, which cannot be obtained, by reason of making and maintaining the railway.

This clause may perhaps apply to minerals lying beyond the specified distance, and which are necessarily left for the lateral support of the railway and works.

Support of ancient buildings by adjoining buildings.

Whether a right to the support of ancient buildings by the adjoining buildings can be acquired by enjoyment, is very doubtful. Such enjoyment will in general be secret, and even if not, there is no way of obstructing it, except by the neighbour who is injured pulling down his

[3] 8 & 9 Vict. c. 20.

house. On the other hand, where the dominant messuage visibly overhangs the adjacent soil, some action may lie,[4] so as to make this an affirmative easement, and therefore to bring it within Lord Tenterden's Act. There is no clear authority on the point; but the tendency of recent decisions is adverse to the acquisition of such an easement by long enjoyment only.[5]

Right of support between buildings by severance.

Mutual rights of support between buildings may, like other rights of the like kind, proceed from an original unity of title. Thus, in *Richards* v. *Rose*,[6] it is said: "We are all of opinion that where houses have been erected in common by the same owner upon a plot of ground, and therefore necessarily requiring mutual support, there is either by a presumed grant, or by a presumed reservation, a right to mutual support; so that the owner who sells one of the houses, as

[4] *Wells* v. *Ody*, 1 M. & W. 452.

[5] *Peyton* v. *Mayor of London*, 9 B. & C. 725; *Brown* v. *Windsor*, 1 Cr. & J. 20; *Chauntler* v. *Robinson*, 19 L. J. Ex. 170; *Solomon* v. *Vintners' Company*, 4 H. & N. 585; *Hargreave* v. *Meade*, 10 Ir. C. L. 117; see *Webb* v. *Bird*, 10 C. B. N. S. 268; 8 Jur. N. S. 621; *Brown* v. *Robins*, 4 H. & N. 186; *Rogers* v. *Taylor*, 2 H. & N. 828.

[6] 9 Exch. 218; see *Peyton* v. *Mayor of London*, 9 B. & C. 725.

CHAP. II. Sect. 4.

against himself, grants such right, and on his own part also reserves the right; and consequently the same mutual dependence of one house upon its neighbour still remains."

Custom of mining.

In *Hilton* v. *Lord Granville*,[7] the defendant claimed under an alleged custom, and also by prescription, the right to do anything that was necessary for the purpose of working mines in a certain manor, making compensation to the tenants for damage done to the surface, but not for damage done to buildings. A jury found the existence of the custom as alleged; but on demurrer in the Queen's Bench, it was said that the custom and prescription claimed were destructive of the substance of the tenant's estate, and that even if a grant could be produced reserving a right in the lord to deprive his grantee of the enjoyment of the thing granted, such a clause must be rejected as repugnant and absurd. The custom and prescription were therefore held to be bad.

This decision maintains its authority as to the

[7] 4 Beav. 130; 1 Cr. & Ph. 283; 5 Q. B. 701; 10 L. J. Ch. 398; 13 L. J. Q. B. 193; *Blackett* v. *Bradley*, 31 L. J. Q. B. 65; see *Grey* v. *Duke of Northumberland*, 13 Ves. 236; 17 Ves. 281; Bainbridge on Mines.

invalidity of the particular custom there in question,[8] although it is now settled that a grant, reserving a right in the grantor to work mines so as to let down the surface granted, is perfectly good.[9]

Statute of Limitations.

In cases of subsidence, the Statute of Limitations begins to run from the time when the damage occurs, and not from the time when the excavation was made.[1]

Sect. 5.

Sect. 5.—VARIOUS NUISANCES.

Other cases of nuisance which have been brought before the Court are :—Obstructions and other Damage to, A Navigable River.[2] A Canal.[3]

[8] *Marquis of Salisbury* v. *Gladstone*, in House of Lords, 9 W. R. 930.

[9] *Rowbotham* v. *Wilson*, 6 E. & B. 593 ; 8 E. & B. 123 ; 8 Cl. 348.

[1] *Nicklin* v. *Williams*, 10 Exch. 259 ; *Bonomi* v. *Backhouse*, E. B. & E. 622 ; in H. L. 9 W. R. 769.

[2] *Attorney-General* v. *Johnson*, 2 Wil. C. C. 87 ; *Priestly* v. *Manchester and Leeds Railway Company*, 2 Rlwy. Ca. 134 ; see *Dobson* v. *Blackmore*, 9 Q. B. 991 ; *Brown* v. *Mallett*, 5 C. B. 599 ; *R.* v. *Haynes*, 7 Ir. L. 2 ; *R.* v. *Ryan*, 8 Ir. L. 119 ; *Dimes* v. *Petty*, 15 Q. B. 276 ; *Abraham* v. *Great Northern Railway Company*, 15 Jur. 895 ; *Hancock* v. *York, Newcastle, and Berwick Railway Company*, 10 C. B. 348 ; *White* v. *Crisp*, 10 Exch. 312 ; *Rose* v. *Mills*, 4 M. & S. 101.

[3] *London and Birmingham Railway Campany* v. *Grand Junction Canal Company*, 1 Rlwy. Ca. 224 ; *Bradbury* v. *Man-*

A Mill Race.[4] A Ferry.[5] A Highway.[6] A Private Right of Way.[7] A Private Siding to a Railway.[8] A Colliery Wayleave.[9] The Entrance

chester and Leeds Railway Company, 5 De G. & Sm. 624; *Case* v. *Midland Railway Company*, 27 Beav. 247.

[4] *Coats* v. *Clarence Railway Company*, 1 Russ. & Myl. 181; *M'Swiney* v. *Haynes*, 1 Eq. 322.

[5] *Churchman* v. *Tunstall*, Hardr. 162; 2 Anst. 608; *Cory* v. *Yarmouth, &c., Railway Company*, 3 Hare, 593; *Huzzey* v. *Field*, 2 C. M. & R. 432; *Giles* v. *Groves*, 6 Dowl. & L. 146; *Blackett* v. *Gillett*, 14 Jur. 814; *Re Cooling*, 14 Jur. 128; *Newton* v. *Cubitt*, 5 C. B. N. S. 627; on another point, C. B. 17th June, 1862; *Leamy* v. *Waterford, &c., Railway Company*, 7 Ir. C. L. 27; *Hemphill* v. *M'Kenna*, 6 Ir. Eq. 57; 8 Ir. L. 43.

[6] *Squire* v. *Campbell*, 1 My. & Cr. 459; *Attorney-General* v. *Forbes*, 2 My. & Cr. 123; *Attorney-General* v. *Manchester and Leeds Railway Company*, 1 Rlwy. Ca. 436; *Spencer* v. *London and Birmingham Railway Company*, 8 Sim. 193; 1 Rlwy. Ca. 159; *Attorney-General* v. *London and Southampton Railway Company*, 1 Rlwy. Ca. 283; *Kemp* v. *London and Brighton Railway Company*, 1 Rlwy. Ca. 495; *Proprietors of Northam Bridge and Roads* v. *London and Southampton Railway Company*, 1 Rlwy. Ca. 653; *Semple* v. *London and Brighton Railway Company*, 1 Rlwy. Ca. 480; *Cunliffe* v. *Whalley*, 13 Beav. 411; *Attorney-General* v. *Sheffield Gas Consumers' Company*, 3 D. M. & G. 341; *Dover Gas Company* v. *Mayor of Dover*, 7 D. M. & G. 545; *R.* v. *Langton Gas Company*, 29 L. J. M. C. 118; *Attorney-General* v. *United Kingdom Electric Telegraph Company*, 10 W. R. 167; 31 L. J. M. C. 166; *R.* v. *Train*, Fos. & Fin. N. P. C. 22, 31 L. J. M. C. 169. See *post*, p. 195.

[7] *Mott* v. *Blackwall Railway Company*, 2 Phil. 632; *Hadfield* v. *Manchester and Leeds Railway Company*, 12 Jur. 1083; *Dorman* v. *Dorman*, 3 Ir. Eq. 385.

[8] *Bell* v. *Midland Railway Company*, 3 D. & J. 673; 10 C. B. N. S. 187.

[9] *Newmarch* v. *Brandling*, 3 Swanst. 99.

to a Vault.[1] A Market.[2] A Right of Stallage.[3] Ground dedicated to Public Recreation.[4] The Construction of a Railway.[5] Also, Damage to Crops.[6]

Some of the foregoing cases will be found more particularly noticed in Chapter IV.

A nuisance in a churchyard comes properly under the cognizance of the Ecclesiastical Courts.[7]

In *Woodman* v. *Robinson*,[8] a parishioner filed a bill against three, not being the whole number of, churchwardens, to restrain them from warming

[1] *Daniel* v. *Anderson*, 10 W. R. 366.

[2] *Anon.*, 2 Ves. S. 414.

[3] *Ellis* v. *Corporation of Bridgnorth*, 2 J. & H. 67.

[4] *Attorney-General* v. *Borough of Southampton*, 1 Giff. 363.

[5] *Great North of England* v. *Clarence Railway Company*, 1 Coll. 507; *London and Birmingham Railway Company* v. *Grand Junction Canal Company*, 1 Rlwy. Ca. 224; *London and Blackwall Railway Company* v. *Limehouse Board of Works*, 3 K. & J. 123; *Hughes* v. *Chester and Holyhead Railway Company*, 1 D. & S. 524.

[6] *Broadbent* v. *Imperial Gas Company*, 7 D. M. &. G. 436; 8 Cl. 600; *Bankart* v. *Houghton*, 5 Jur. N. S. 282; 27 Beav. 425; Ll. Jj. 21st July, 1862; *Williams* v. *Earl Jersey*, Cr. & Ph. 91.

[7] *Large* v. *Alton*, Cro. Jac. 462; *Wenmouth* v. *Collins*, 2 Lord Raymond, 850; *Quilter* v. *Newtown*, Carth. 151; *Wilson* v. *M'Neath*, 3 B. & Ald. 245; 3 Phillimore, 89; *Buxton* v. *Calcote*, *Cade* v. *Newnham*, 3 Phillimore, 91.

[8] 2 Sim. N. S. 204.

CHAP. II.
Sect. 5.

the church in a manner which he alleged to be injurious to health. Lord Cranworth, V.-C., considered it very doubtful whether a single individual could sustain such a bill, but it was not necessary to decide the point.[9]

[9] For Nuisances to Dwelling Houses see page 122. Whilst these sheets were passing through the press an Act was passed empowering the Court of Chancery to try the legal rights in all cases. See Appendix.

CHAPTER III.

TRESPASS.

1. *Jurisdiction.*
2. *Taking part of the substance of the Inheritance.*
3. *Lord of a Manor and Copyholders.*
4. *Various acts of Trespass.*
5. *Protection of Real Property during litigation.*

Sect. 1.—JURISDICTION.

Sect. 1.

Definition of trespass.

AN illegal entry upon, or immediate injury to, real property corporeal in possession is trespass.[1]

Jurisdiction formerly not exercised.

The jurisdiction of the Court to grant injunctions was formerly not exercised in cases of pure trespass.[2]

Early instances.

This rule was first relaxed in cases where the

[1] Chit. Prec. Pl., 2nd edit. p. 703. As to the distinction between an immediate and an indirect injury, see *Reynolds* v. *Clarke*, 2 Lord Raymond, 1399; *Scott* v. *Shepherd*, 1 Sm. Lead. Ca.; *Scott* v. *Nelson*, 5 Ir. L. 207.

[2] *Coulson* v. *White*, 3 Atk. 21; *Mogg* v. *Mogg*, 2 Dick. 670; *Mortimer* v. *Cottrill*, 2 Cox, 205; *Pillsworth* v. *Hopton*, 6 Ves. 51; *Smith* v. *Collyer*, 8 Ves. 89; *Norway* v. *Rowe*, 19 Ves. 146.

party complaining being in undisputed possession of a close, a wrong-doer was attempting to take away part of the substance of the inheritance, such as coal or timber, or to do other irreparable mischief.[3] It was said[4] by Lord Eldon, that, "The distinction, long ago established, was, that, if a person, still living, committed a trespass by cutting timber, or taking lead ore, or coal, this Court would not interfere; but gave the discovery; and then an action might be brought for the value discovered: but, the trespass dying with the person, if he died, the Court said, this being property, there must be an account of the value; though the law gave no remedy.[5] In that instance, therefore, the account was given, where an injunction was not wanted. Throughout Lord Hardwicke's time, and down to that of Lord Thurlow, the distinction between waste and trespass was acknowledged: and I have frequently alluded to the

[3] *Mitchell* v. *Dors*, 6 Ves. 147; *Robinson* v. *Lord Byron*, 1 Bro. C. C. 588; 2 Cox, 4; *Hanson* v. *Gardiner*, 7 Ves. 308; *Talbot* v. *Hope Scott*, 4 K. & J. 122.

[4] *Thomas* v. *Oakley*, 18 Ves. 186.

[5] *The Marquis of Lansdowne* v. *The Marchioness of Lansdowne*, 1 Mad. 116.

case[6] upon which Lord Thurlow first hesitated: a person, having a close demised to him, began to get coal there; but continued to work under the contiguous close, belonging to another person; and it was held, that the former, as waste, would be restrained; but as to the close, which was not demised to him, it was a mere trespass; and the Court did not interfere: but I take it, that Lord Thurlow changed his opinion upon that, holding, that if the defendant was taking the substance of the inheritance, the liberty of bringing an action was not all the relief to which, in equity, he was entitled. The interference of the Court is to prevent your removing that which is his estate. Upon that principle Lord Thurlow granted the injunction as to both. That has since been repeatedly followed, and whether it was trespass under the colour of another's right actually existing or not."

Trespass under colour of title.

Usually the acts of trespass complained of have originated in some confusion of boundaries,[7] or otherwise, under what is called "a colour of

6 *Flamang's Case*, see post.

7 *Bateman* v. *Johnson*, Fitzgib. 106; *Kinder* v. *Jones*, 17 Ves. 110.

Chap. III. Sect. 1. Davenport v. Davenport.

title," the meaning of which phrase is thus explained[8] by Wigram, V.-C.: "The jurisdiction of the Court in cases of injunction, originally, no doubt, arose in cases of waste where there was privity between the parties. All the earlier cases are of that description. The Court began afterwards to interfere in cases of trespass; but I believe it will be found that the cases in which the jurisdiction was exercised in restraining trespass, have been cases of this peculiar description—the party complaining has been in possession of property, and has complained that his possession was wrongfully invaded by some alleged trespasser. The alleged trespasser, on the other hand, has not admitted the possession of the plaintiff, nor claimed a right to invade such possession as he had, nor intended to do so, as in the case of the underground workings of adjoining mines, and the Court has distinguished these cases from ordinary cases of trespass, by saying the alleged wrong-doer claimed under colour of title. The cases of railway companies taking lands, under the compulsory powers given

[8] *Davenport* v. *Davenport*, 7 Hare, 217.

them by parliament, are of the same class. Neither party disputes the abstract right of the other to that which he claims. The dispute is as to the practical application of the law to the facts of the case. It has always appeared to me, the Court was trying to get out of a technical rule, with a view to the better protection of property.

Lady Bastard's case.

"I remember a case concerning the property of Lady Bastard, in the West of England, in which some observations on this point were made by the Lord Chancellor in the course of the argument. Persons working mines insisted that, within a particular district, there was a right common to all miners to make drifts through private closes, for the purpose of draining the mines. This right they were about to assert by cutting a trench through some property of Lady Bastard. In that case the Lord Chancellor granted the injunction."[9]

Special circumstances.

Such circumstances as that the trespass is carried on secretly underground or aboveground by collusion with a tenant, have been considered

[9] *Attorney-General* v. *United Kingdom Electric Telegraph Company*, 10 W. R. 167; *Selby* v. *Crystal Palace Gas Company*, 10 W. R. 432, 636.

CHAP. III. Sect. 1.

to aid the jurisdiction, as it appears that a case of simple open aggression is more properly dealt with in other courts.[1]

Trespass by adverse claimants.

Recently, a claimant who had not brought ejectment was restrained from cutting sods, timber, &c., which he had threatened to do in assertion of his alleged ownership;[2] in an earlier case,[3] where a claimant had been non-suited in an ejectment, the Court refused to interfere to prevent him from vexatiously distraining on, or otherwise molesting the tenants.

Protection of an estate during litigation.

There remain to be considered the cases in which a party claiming an estate of which he was clearly out of possession, has endeavoured to prevent his adversary, who was in possession, and insisted upon a title to that possession, from cutting timber or doing other acts of destruction before the right could be tried at law.[4]

Claimant out of possession.

It seems that a party so circumstanced cannot at the time maintain an action of trespass, but if

[1] *Talbot* v. *Hope Scott*, 4 K. & J. 122; *Best* v. *Drake*, 11 Hare, 369; see *Deere* v. *Guest*, 1 Myl. & Cr. 516.

[2] *Lowndes* v. *Bettle*, V.-C. K., 12th June, 1862.

[3] *Best* v *Drake*, 11 Hare, 369; see *Hodgson* v. *Duce*, 2 Jur. N. S. 1014.

[4] See *Webster* v. *South Eastern Railway Company*, 1 Sim. N.S. 272, and post, 196.

the subsequently establishes his title he may then recover damages for the past wrong.[5] So, as a general rule, in the case of a party out of possession of an estate claiming equitable relief, the right to which depends upon the right of possession, the Court requires that the party so circumstanced should recover the possession before he files his bill for the consequential equitable relief.[6]

Timber cut destructively.

After many ineffectual attempts to induce the Court to extend to real property, pending litigation, the measure of protection which is constantly afforded to personalty, an injunction was at last granted in a case where the defendant had cut down timber in a manner so destructive that it could not be referred to any fair act of ownership.[7]

Acts which will be restrained.

As to the character of the acts which the Court will interfere to restrain, it has been said[8] by Wigram, V.-C.—" The jurisdiction of the Courts

[5] *Butcher* v. *Butcher*, 7 B. & C. 399; *Turner* v. *Cameron Coal Company*, 5 Exch. 932; *Lichfield* v. *Ready*, 5 Exch. 939; *Barnett* v. *Guildford*, 11 Exch. 19.

[6] *Vice* v. *Thomas*, 4 Y. & C. 560.

[7] *Neale* v. *Cripps*, 4 K. & J. 472.

[8] *North Union Railway Company* v. *The Bolton and Preston Railway Company*, 3 Rlwy. Ca. 345.

CHAP. III. Sect. I.

to grant injunctions in cases of pure trespass is comparatively of modern establishment. But it is now clearly settled that in cases of trespass under colour of title, where the mischief apprehended is irreparable, the jurisdiction of the Court exists; and I incline strongly to the opinion, that whether the mischief be irreparable or not, this Court ought by decree at least, if not upon motion, to extend and apply the jurisdiction of preventive justice to all cases of trespass in which (by analogy to cases of specific performance), damages would be an inadequate and uncertain remedy, and the protection of a right in specie the only mode of doing complete justice between the parties."[9]

Sect. 2.

Sect. 2.—TAKING AWAY THE SUBSTANCE OF THE INHERITANCE.

Mining.

Lord Eldon often spoke of *Flamang's Case*[1] as the first instance of an injunction to restrain

[9] *Attorney-General* v. *Sheffield Gas Consumers' Company*, 3 D. M. G. 321.

[1] 6 Ves. 147; 7 Ves. 308; 15 Ves. 138; 18 Ves. 186; see *Emmott* v. *Mitchell*, 14 Sim. 432.

trespass. There a person, landlord of two closes, had let one to a tenant who took coal out of that close, and also out of the other which was not demised. The former as waste might of course be restrained, and ultimately after some hesitation Lord Thurlow granted the injunction as to both.

Working out of bounds.

This was soon followed by cases where the adjacent owners being altogether strangers in title, one of them had worked as it is called "out of bounds," into the minerals of his neighbour.[2]

Powell *v.* Aiken.

In the important case of *Powell* v. *Aiken*,[3] the plaintiffs were lessees of certain beds of coal lying between two collieries which were vested in the defendant Garratt, and had been mortgaged by him to a banking company, who were also made defendants. Garratt whilst in possession had secretly made a large aircourse and certain level roads through the plaintiff's mine in order to connect his two collieries, and had fraudulently removed large quantities of the plaintiff's coal in

[2] *Earl of Lonsdale* v. *Curwen*, 3 Bli. 168; *Mitchell* v. *Dors*, 6 Ves. 147; *Walker* v. *Fletcher*, 3 Bli. 172; and see *Grey* v. *Duke of Northumberland*, 17 Ves. 281; *Haigh* v. *Jaggar*, 2 Coll. 231.

[3] 4 K. & J. 343.

so doing. The mortgagees, who were not privy to these acts, afterwards took possession and continued to use the aircourse and level roads, and, as it was alleged, abstracted further quantities of the plaintiff's coal. Wood, V.-C., decided that the mortgagor and mortgagees respectively were answerable for the market value at the pit's mouth of all coal removed or gotten whilst they were respectively in possession, without prejudice to any question as to which of them was responsible for coal, the precise times of getting or removing which could not be ascertained. An injunction was granted to restrain the defendants from taking away the plaintiff's coal, and from continuing to use the aircourse and roads.

His Honour held that he could not throw upon the banking company the expense of filling up the aircourse or removing the roads, as they did not make them,[4] and also that the Court could not decree compensation to the plaintiff for the severance of his mine and his being obliged to leave additional barriers, nor charge the defen-

[4] *Clegg* v. *Dearden*, 12 Q. B. 576.

dants with a wayleave rent in respect of the use of the said aircourse aud roads.[5]

Delay.

We have already noticed that parties asking the Court to interfere with mining operations are especially bound to be prompt in making their application.[6]

Timber.

In *Courthope* v. *Mapplesden* and *Hamilton* v. *Worsefold*, a trespasser was restrained from cutting timber in collusion with the plaintiff's tenants.[7] And in another case an injunction was granted on a bill filed by trustees tenants in fee simple upon trust to sell, to restrain the defendant from cutting down trees in a lane which the plaintiffs claimed as belonging to them, but which the defendant averred to be part of the waste of a manor of which he was lord.[8]

Stone.

So with regard to quarrying stone. In *Thomas* v. *Oakley*,[9] the bill stated that the plaintiff was seised in fee simple of an estate in which there was a stone quarry; and the defendant having a

5 See now 21 & 22 Vict. c. 27, s. 2.

6 *Norway* v. *Rowe*, 19 Ves. 144; *Field* v. *Beaumont*, 1 Swanst. 208; ante, Chap. I. sect. 5.

7 10 Ves. 290; see *Smith* v. *Collyer*, 8 Ves. 89; *Haigh* v. *Jaggar*, 2 Coll. 236.

8 *Kinder* v. *Jones*, 17 Ves. 110.

9 18 Ves. 184.

CHAP. III. Sect. 2.

contiguous estate, with a right to enter the plaintiff's quarry and take stone for certain limited purposes, had entered and taken stone for other purposes, and it prayed for an injunction and account. Lord Eldon, in overruling a demurrer, said—"If this protection would be granted in the case of timber, coals, or lead-ore, why is it not equally to be applied to a quarry? The comparative value cannot be considered. The present established course is to sustain a bill for the purpose of injunction, connecting it with the account in both cases; and not to put the plaintiff to come here for an injunction and to go to law for damages."

Stones, shingle, &c.

Orders have also been made to restrain the removal from the sea-shore of stones valuable from their rarity, or of stones, shingle, &c., which formed a protection against the encroachments of the sea.[1]

Cutting turf.

In some Irish cases injunctions have been granted to restrain the cutting of turf, where the defendants, being tenants of the plaintiff, were cutting on a neighbouring bog belonging to their

[1] *Earl Cowper* v. *Baker*, 17 Ves. 128; *Clowes* v. *Beck*, 13 Beav. 347.

landlord; but the jurisdiction has apparently not been exercised at present in a case of mere trespass.[2]

Sect. 3.—LORD OF A MANOR AND COPYHOLDERS.

Sect. 3.

Lord of the manor as plaintiff. Enclosure.

Under the Statute of Merton,[3] the lord of a manor had authority to enclose part of the common, provided that he left sufficient for pasture, &c., for the tenants. There are early precedents of bills to establish this right against the tenants, and to restrain them from trespassing on the part so enclosed.[4]

Copyholder cutting timber under claim of estovers.

A case which appears to have been one of trespass was cited in *Mogg* v. *Mogg*.[5] The plaintiff was lord of a manor upon which the defendants claimed a right to take estovers, and under that right they cut down timber in one day to the value

[2] *Sandys* v. *Murray*, 1 Ir. Eq. 29; *Lowe* v. *Lucey*, 1 Ir. Eq. 93; *Wrixon* v. *Condran*, 1 Ir. Eq. 380; *Congleton* v. *Mitchell*, 12 Ir. Eq. 34.

[3] 20 Hen. 3, c. 4.

[4] *Weekes* v. *Slake*, 2 Vern. 301; *Arthington* v. *Fowkes*, 2 Vern. 356; *Hanson* v. *Gardiner*, 7 Ves. 305.

[5] 2 Dick. 670.

Chap. III. Sect. 3.

of 400*l*. Upon these facts, Camden, L. C., granted an injunction.

Mines.

And after the lord of a manor had sold it, he obtained an injunction to restrain the purchaser from opening mines which were reserved out of the conveyance.[6]

Copyholder plaintiff.

So, conversely, a copyholder is entitled to the interference of the Court to prevent the lord from

Timber and coal.

felling timber on the copyhold tenement, or getting coal lying under it.[7]

Confusion of boundaries.

We have already noticed a case in which the defendant was restrained from cutting down trees standing in a private lane, which the plaintiffs claimed as part of their fee simple estate, and the defendant averred to be part of the waste of a manor of which he was the lord.[8]

Forfeiture.

The Court of Chancery has also jurisdiction to relieve a copyholder against an illegal seizure of the copyhold property by the lord of the manor.[9]

[6] *Gibson* v. *Smith*, 2 Atk. 182.

[7] *Grey* v. *Duke of Northumberland*, 13 Ves. 236; 17 Ves. 281; *Bourne* v. *Taylor*, 10 East, 189; *Lewis* v. *Branthwaite*, 2 B. & Ad. 437; *Whitechurch* v. *Holworthy*, 19 Ves. 213; 4 Maul. & Sel. 340; see *Hilton* v. *Lord Granville*, 4 Beav. 130; 1 C. & P. 283; 5 Q. B. 701; *Bowser* v. *Maclean*, 2 D. F. J. 415.

[8] *Kinder* v. *Jones*, 17 Ves. 110.

[9] *Andrews* v. *Hulse*, 4 K. & J. 392.

Sect. 4.—VARIOUS ACTS OF TRESPASS.

Sect. 4.

Interfering with a stream.

In the early case of *Robinson* v. *Lord Byron*,[1] the defendant, who had large pieces of water in his park, supplied by a stream which flowed to the plaintiff's mill, at one time stopped the water, and at another let it go in such quantities as to endanger the mill, his object being to extort money. An injunction was granted to restrain him from preventing the water from flowing in regular quantities to the mill on the ground of the irreparable mischief that would have been done before there could have been any trial at law.

Shingle protecting the shore.

In *Clowes* v. *Beck*,[2] the plaintiff alleged that he was seised of a tract of land between high and low water mark, from which the defendants had carted away a great quantity of shingle and sand for the purpose of repairing the highway, and that the consequence would be that the sea would encroach upon the plaintiff's lands, upon which

[1] 1 Bro. C. C. 588; 2 Cox, 4; 7 Ves. 308. This has been spoken of as a case of nuisance (*Blakemore* v. *Glamorganshire Canal Company*, 1 My. & K. 184), but see *Courtney* v. *Collett*, 1 Ld. Raymond, 272.

[2] 13 Beav. 347.

CHAP. III. Sect. 4.

his mansion house stood, to his great and irreparable injury. The answer denied the plaintiff's title, and that any injury would ensue, and justified under certain Acts of Parliament. An injunction was granted before the legal right was determined.

Vendor and purchaser.

A purchaser who has got into possession before paying his purchase money, and a vendor remaining in possession after the contract, will not be allowed to commit any waste or destruction;[3] and although the Court is reluctant to interfere against a party in possession under a claim of a legal title, yet if he has gained possession by fraud, an injunction against waste will be granted and a receiver of the rents and profits appointed.[4]

Party in possession under claim of legal title.

Right of way.

There are several precedents for restraining the exercise of a pretended right of way claimed under colour of title. Thus, in an early case,[5] the vendor

[3] *Crockford* v. *Alexander*, 15 Ves. 138; *Lloyd* v. *Passingham*, 16 Ves. 65; *Norway* v. *Rowe*, 19 Ves. 155; *Petley* v. *Eastern Counties Railway Company*, 8 Sim. 483; *Webster* v. *South Eastern Railway Company*, 1 Sim. N.S. 274. If a purchaser has bought under a decree, it seems that he may be restrained on motion, although not a party to the cause; *Casamajor* v. *Strode*, 1 S. & S. 381.

[4] *Lloyd* v. *Passingham*, 16 Ves. 59; *Lloyd* v. *Lord Trimleston*, 2 Moll. 81; *Talbot* v. *Hope Scott*, 4 K. & J. 96; and see post, Sect. 5.

[5] *Pit* v. *Lady Claverinth*, 1 Barn. K. B. 318. The reservation

of a manor reserved to himself and his heirs a convenient wayleave, such as he and his heirs should think proper, for the carriage of coals from certain works to the Tyne. The defendant was the lessee of the vendor, and under colour of the reservation she made a waggon-way with planks, according to a custom which had come into use in the north at that time. Upon this a bill was filed against her, raising the question whether a waggon-way was within the reservation of a way-leave. The Barons of the Exchequer and the Lord Chancellor appear to have differed in opinion upon the legal question, but no objection was made to the jurisdiction.

Deere *v.* Guest.

In *Deere* v. *Guest,*[o] the bill stated that the defendants had constructed a tram-road across the plaintiff's land without his knowledge, having first obtained by fraud the consent of one who was then occupying the premises as a yearly tenant. The plaintiff did not discover the

of a sufficient wayleave justifies the construction of a railway; *Farrow* v. *Vansittart,* 1 Rlwy. Ca. 602; *Barnard* v. *Wallis,* 2 Rlwy. Ca. 162; *Dand* v. *Kingscote,* 6 M. & W. 174; *Bishop* v. *North,* 11 M. & W. 418; and see *Hughes* v. *Chester and Holyhead Railway Company,* 1 Dr. & S. 524, on appeal 10 W. R. 219.

[o] 1 Myl. & Cr. 516; *Perks* v. *Wycombe Railway Company,* V.-C. S. 10 W. R. 788.

existence of the road until the defendants had been using it for nearly three years. The tenancy determined about a month after the discovery was made, and the plaintiff shortly afterwards sent workmen to restore the land to its former condition, but this they were forcibly prevented from doing. The bill prayed that the defendants might be restrained from using the road or interrupting the plaintiff's workmen, and that they might be decreed to restore the lands to their former condition. A demurrer was allowed, Lord Cottenham saying—"The thing here complained of has been done, the tram-road has, with the leave of the tenant in possession, been completed, and the Court is asked by the bill to restrain the defendants, who, having finished the undertaking, are now in the daily use and occupation of it, from continuing so to use it, and from interrupting the servants and workmen of the plaintiff in their attempt to destroy it; in other words, the Court is asked virtually to eject the defendants, and authorise the plaintiffs themselves to take possession of the tram-road. The case originally may have been a case of waste,—waste occasioned by the cutting of the tramroad, and the laying of the iron rails over the plaintiff's land, but what is now claimed by the defendants is simply a right of way, and if they are not entitled to that right, they are mere trespassers, and the plaintiffs have their proper legal remedy against them as such." It will be observed, that the case made by the bill was one of fraudulent invasion of the plaintiff's right, and that there was no allegation that the defendants claimed to do what they had done under any pretence of title.

Running powers.

The succeeding authorities illustrate clearly the principle upon which the jurisdiction rests. In the *North Union Railway Company* v. *Bolton and Preston Railway Company*,[7] the defendants had certain parliamentary powers of using the plaintiffs' station, and passing along and across their line of railway. The object of the bill was to restrain them from using these powers in a manner alleged to be excessive. Wigram, V.-C., after asserting (in a passage which has been already cited) the jurisdiction of the court to restrain a trespass under colour of title, enter-

[7] 3 Rlwy. Ca. 345.

CHAP. III. Sect. 4.

tained a motion for an injunction, but ordered it to stand over that an action might be brought.

Tramway in a mine.

So in *Powell* v. *Aiken*,[8] the defendants were ordered to discontinue the use of a road which they had improperly made through the plaintiff's minerals.

Lastly, we have the case of *Bowser* v. *Maclean*.[9] There the plaintiff was a copyholder, and the defendant the lessee of all the minerals on the manor. He was entitled to make a tramway through the minerals under the plaintiff's land, and to carry along it any coals which he might dig within the limits of the manor. The bill averred that the defendant drove along this tramway coals which he dug in a colliery in his occupation beyond the limits of the manor, and also that he had broken ways under the plaintiff's land for ventilating the last-mentioned colliery.

The defendant demurred, arguing that the plaintiffs were confined to a legal remedy. Campbell, L. C., overruled the demurrer, saying, "In considering this objection, we must bear in mind that the bill complains of a secret and

[8] 4 K. & J. 343.
[9] 2 D. F. & J. 415.

clandestine use of the railway; that the defendant is charged with making a profit by this surreptitious use of the way, and that the bill contains the statement of the defendant having broken the soil in the mines under Cockton Hill estate, belonging to the plaintiffs, for the purpose of making a communication between these mines and another mine in his occupation beyond the limits of the manor, and having ventilated this mine with air from the mines within the manor, obtained by the barrier between them being thus broken.[1] Can it be said that all this is a mere dry trespass, for which a court of equity will supply no remedy?"

Parliamentary powers. Canal and railway companies.

The cases which have arisen upon the proceedings of canal, railway, and other companies authorised by Parliament to interfere with the rights of landowners, will be considered in the next chapter.

Gas and Telegraph companies.

There seems to be little doubt that in a proper case, the owner of the soil is entitled to an injunction to prevent a company from breaking

[1] See *Lady Eastard's Case*, cited in *Davenport* v. *Davenport*, 7 Hare, 217.

CHAP. III.
Sect. 4.

up a road to insert gas-pipes, telegraph wires, posts, &c., although the damage is only slight.[2]

Three years peaceable possession.

According to an old practice, when a party had been three years in peaceable possession of a close, he could have an injunction of course to prevent an adverse claimant from entering, before the hearing of the cause. The last instance of such an injunction is said to be where[3] Lord Hardwicke restrained certain commissioners of turnpikes from forcibly entering the plaintiff's garden and digging gravel there, saying that it was the case of Naboth's vineyard.

Sect. 5.

Sect. 5.—PROTECTION OF REAL PROPERTY DURING LITIGATION.

Injunction or Receiver.

The protection sought may be an injunction to restrain the party in possession from committing spoil or destruction, or a receiver to hold the accruing rents for the party who shall ultimately be successful in the litigation. Neither will,

[2] *Attorney-General* v. *United Kingdom Railway Company*, 10 W. R. 167; *Selby* v. *Crystal Palace Gas Company*, 10 W. R. 432, 636. See ante, p. 172.

[3] *Hughes* v. *Trustees of Morden College*, 1 Ves. sen. 188; Eden on Injunctions, 334.

however, be granted, except under special circumstances.[4]

Injunction, *Smith* v. *Collyer*.

In *Smith* v. *Collyer*,[5] a motion was made by a devisee to restrain the heir-at-law from cutting timber, the validity of the devise being disputed. Lord Eldon refused it, saying, that he did not recollect any instance of the kind. In a subsequent case,[6] Sir William Grant, M. R., after noticing that no case had been cited in which the Court had interfered for such a purpose, at the suit of either the heir or a devisee, added: "One should think the case of the devisee a stronger one than that of the heir; because till the will is set aside, the *primâ facie* title is in the devisee."[7] "I own I cannot see a very good

Jones v. *Jones*.

[4] *Knight* v. *Duplessis*, 2 Ves. sen., 360; see ante, p. 180; *Webster* v. *South Eastern Railway Company*, 1 Sim. N.S. 272.

[5] 8 Ves. 89. It is not clear whether Lord Eldon considered the plaintiffs or the defendant to be in possession. See *Norway* v. *Rowe*, 19 Ves. 155, and *Haigh* v. *Jaggar*, 2 Coll. 236.

[6] *Jones* v. *Jones*, 3 Mer. 173.

[7] Contr. Sir Anthony Hart in *Lloyd* v. *Lord Trimleston*, 2 Moll. 83. "On the death of the ancestor, the heir has title to enter and retain possession until the Court interferes. If it be said that the devisee being let into possession by the favour of the occupiers acquires any right, that would be to adjust the possession according to the will and pleasure of mere casual persons who happened to be the occupying tenants at the death of the testator. But my opinion of the law is this, that the heir has upon the instant of the death of his ancestor in pos-

CHAP. III. Sect. 5.

reason why the Court which interferes for the preservation of personal property pending a suit in the Ecclesiastical Court, should not interpose to preserve real property pending a suit concerning the validity of the devise." "If the Court will not interpose to stay waste, *à fortiori* will it refuse to appoint a receiver, or to restrain the devisee from exercising other acts of ownership over the property?"

Lord Fingal v. *Blake.*

A step in advance was made in an Irish case, *Lord Fingal* v. *Blake.*[8] This was a bill by a devisee in trust against the heir-at-law, who was in possession, and had taken an assignment of a tenant's interest in part of the lands. An in-

Injunction.

junction against waste, which had been refused by Lord Chancellor Manners on an interlocutory motion, was granted at the hearing by Lord Chancellor Hart. The heir then declined to try an issue *devisavit vel non*, but he still retained possession, and claimed a beneficial interest under a

session a right to enter, and turn out by the shoulders any other person, except only the widow, who has a right to stay until her dower is assigned to her." See, however, *Talbot* v. *Hope Scott*, 4 K. & J. 117.

[8] 2 Moll. 542; 1 Moll. 113, 158; 2 Moll. 50; and see *Lloyd* v. *Lord Trimleston*, 2 Moll. 83.

Receiver.

resulting trust. He had formerly been appointed receiver by consent; but on a further hearing, an application was made that a different receiver might be appointed. The Lord Chancellor Hart now said:[9] "I have long doubted the soundness of the old decisions with respect to waste. I think the Court has jurisdiction to restrain waste by the heir disputing the will of real estate, and will do so at any time on motion.

"The title of the heir-at-law against the dispositions of the will, must, as he now admits the devise to the trustees legally speaking to be good, be by virtue of a resulting trust. But before either the heir-at-law or the devisees, whichever is entitled, can take in possession, certain antecedent temporary trusts are to be executed. Where a will is disputed by the heir-at-law, and he is in possession, it requires a strong case to take away the rents from the heir-at-law whilst the will is disputed; but in a strong case the Court will do it. It will prevent injury to the devisee. We know that by the old practice on this point, plaintiff stating that defendant claimed

[9] 2 Moll. 60.

by an adverse title, stated himself out of Court, and the Court has continued to be reluctant to remove an heir contesting the will; but not in the same way to grant an injunction against waste about to be committed by him. I have no doubt that the Court will now in such a case readily exercise its powers to prevent irreparable injury to the property. It would be absurd to abstain from doing so out of consideration to the heir. Suppose a case in which the matter in litigation was a valuable house, a mansion valuable for its antiquity, or for other reasons not capable of being measured in money, if the heir may, pending the suit, pull down the house, and considering the spirit of such suits we may put very strong suppositions, he would have it in his power to make the cause, perhaps in the principal point, not worth the following. There is a marked distinction between cases for a receiver, and for an injunction against waste." Under the circumstances of that case a receiver was granted.

Clark v. *Dew.* Receiver.

Shortly afterwards in England an interlocutory motion,[1] by devisees under a will which had been

[1] *Clark* v. *Dew*, 1 Russ. & Myl. 103.

already decided to be invalid as a disposition of personal estate, for a receiver against the heir, was of course refused. And subsequently in two cases, in which *Fingal* v. *Blake* was unfortunately not cited, the Court refused to restrain a litigant in possession from committing irreparable injury, on the ground of the absence of precedent.[2] However, in *Anwyl* v. *Owens*,[3] where an heir *ex parte paterna* brought ejectment against an heir *ex parte materna*, and then filed a bill and moved *ex parte* for an injunction to restrain the fall and sale of timber, K. Bruce, L. J., said: "As this application has for its object to preserve property during litigation, we are both of opinion that it will be proper to grant, and we accordingly grant, an interim order to restrain the sale, and all other acts to restrain which this bill was filed, until the motion for an injunction is disposed of." The plaintiff gave an undertaking as to damages.

Haigh v. *Jaggar.*

Davenport v. *Davenport.*

Anwyl v. *Owens.*

Injunction.

In *Talbot* v. *Hope Scott*,[4] most of the preceding

Result of authorities as to ap-

[2] *Haigh* v. *Jaggar*, 2 Coll. 231; *Davenport* v. *Davenport*, 7 Hare, 217.

[3] 22 L. J. Ch. 995.

[4] 4 K. & J. 96; see *Wright* v. *Wilkin*, 7 W. R. 337, 431.

CHAP. III.
Sect. 5.
pointing a receiver.
Talbot v. Hope Scott.

authorities were reviewed, and with respect to granting a receiver, Wood, V.-C., said: "The result is, that I can neither find any semblance of authority, nor can I conceive any rational ground upon principle, for holding that where one person is in the possession of the rents and profits, claiming to be the holder by a simple legal title, and another person claims to hold by a like legal title, the former can be ousted in this Court, until that legal title has been finally determined at law;" but his Honour intimated that there might be flagrant acts of what the Court calls in some instances malicious waste—acts which no man, as mere owner in ordinary possession of the property would do, but indicating on the face of them fraud, in which the Court would interfere by injunction.

Injunction to restrain malicious waste.
Neale v. Cripps.

This suggestion was acted upon in *Neale* v. *Cripps*,[5] where the heir-at-law, after ejectment brought against persons claiming through the devisees, moved for an injunction to restrain them from cutting down any timber or timber-like trees, standing or growing on the estate,

[5] 4 K. & J. 472.

and from removing therefrom, or disposing of, any timber or timber-like trees which might already be cut, and from committing any other waste. The defendants did not appear upon the motion.

Evidence.

By an affidavit filed on behalf of the plaintiff, it was deposed as follows: "The said defendants have lately caused the timber and timber-like trees on the said estate to be cut down, and, to a considerable extent, since the said action of ejectment has been commenced, and they are proceeding to cause the remainder of the trees on the said estate, which are of any value, to be cut down; and the said defendants, or their said solicitors, have cut down the timber standing on the said estate in such manner and to such extent, as nearly to strip the land of all trees and timber-like trees thereon of any value; and I believe that the said defendants have cut down the said timber, and are proceeding to cut down the remainder thereof, for the express purpose of wasting the value of the property of the plaintiff in the said estate, and with intent to defraud the plaintiff of his just right in the said estate; for the way in which the said timber is cut is so destructive, that it cannot be referred to any fair act of ownership."

Upon this evidence an injunction was granted.

Quare impedit.

In an old case an incumbent was prohibited, pending a *quare impedit*, from felling timber upon the glebe, and upon the lands of copyholders holding of a manor parcel of the rectory.[6]

[6] *Drury* v. *Kent*, Hob. 36; 2 Rol. Abr. 813.

CHAPTER IV.

CONSTRUCTION OF PUBLIC WORKS.

Sect. 1.—GENERAL CONSIDERATIONS.

Sect. 1.

Action at law upon a statute.

As a general principle,[1] where a statute prohibits the doing of a particular act affecting the public, no person has a right of action against another merely because he has done the prohibited act. It is incumbent on the party complaining to allege and prove that the doing of the act prohibited has caused him some special damage, some peculiar injury beyond that which

Special damage.

[1] *Chamberlaine* v. *Chester and Birkenhead Railway Company*, 1 Exch. 870.

CHAP. IV. Sect. 1.

he may be supposed to sustain in common with the rest of the Queen's subjects by an infringement of the law. But where the act prohibited is obviously prohibited for the protection of a particular party, there it is not necessary to allege special damage.[2]

Jurisdiction in Equity to enforce the provisions of a statute.

The Court of Chancery has no general jurisdiction to enforce the provisions of an Act of Parliament.[3] Rights arising under it will be dealt with according to ordinary rules and principles, and therefore where there is no irreparable mischief or other special circumstance, the parties will be left to their remedies at law.[4] The rule that the party complaining is bound to show special damage applies strongly to injunction suits, where it is necessary (except perhaps in

Irreparable mischief.

Special damage.

[2] *Lee* v. *Milner*, 2 Y. & C. Exch. 618 ; *Corporation of Liverpool* v. *Chorley Water Works*, 2 D. M. G. 852 ; *Warden, &c., Dover Harbour* v. *The South Eastern Railway Company*, 9 Hare, 489 ; *The Cromford and High Peak Railway Company* v. *Stockport, Disley, &c., Railway Company*, 1 D. & J. 326.

[3] This is the province of the Court of Queen's Bench by writ of Mandamus ; as to which, see Hodges' Law of Railways, 640.

[4] *Weale* v. *West Middlesex Water Works Company*, 1 J. & W. 371 ; *Attorney-General* v. *Corporation of Liverpool*, 1 My. & Cr. 171 ; *Attorney-General* v. *Birmingham Railway Company*, 3 Mac. & Gor. 453.

proceedings at the instance of the Attorney-General) that the damage should be what is called substantial.[5] But in giving relief to a single proprietor, the fact that a large class may suffer unless his rights are invaded will not be taken into consideration.[6]

Nature of parliamentary powers.

The questions which we have to consider in this chapter are mainly those which arise between landowners and persons who have obtained parliamentary powers to construct canals, railways, &c. The relation between such persons or corporations and the landowners along the line of their works is now clearly settled. In *Blakemore* v. *Glamorganshire Canal Company*,[7] Lord Eldon said, "When I look upon these Acts of Parliament, I consider them all in the light of contracts made by the legislature, on behalf of

Blakemore v. Glamorganshire Canal Company.

[5] *Corporation of Liverpool* v. *Chorley Water Works*, 2 D. M. G. 852; *Ware* v. *Regent's Canal Company*, 3 D. & J. 212; *The Cromford and High Peak Railway Company* v. *The Stockport, &c., Railway Company*, 1 D. & J. 326; *Holyoake* v. *Shrewsbury and Birmingham Railway Company*, 5 Rlwy. Ca. 421; *Wintle* v. *Bristol and South Wales Union Railway Company*, 10 W. R. 210; *Wandsworth Board of Works* v. *London and South Western Railway*, 8 Jur. N. S. 691.

[6] *Broadbent* v. *Imperial Gas Company*, 7 D. M. G. 462; *Attorney-General* v. *Borough of Birmingham*, 4 K. & J. 528.

[7] 1 Myl. & K. 162. As regarded Mr. Blakemore the statute was compulsory.

every person interested in anything to be done under them; and I have no hesitation in asserting that, unless that principle is applied in construing statutes of this description, they will become instruments of greater oppression than anything in the whole system of administration under our constitution. Such Acts of Parliament have now become extremely numerous; and from their number and operation, they so much affect individuals, that I apprehend those who come for them to Parliament, do, in effect, undertake that they shall do and submit to whatever the legislature empowers and compels them to do; and that they do nothing else:—that they shall do and shall forbear all that they are required to do and to forbear, as well with reference to the interests of the public, as with reference to the interests of individuals." Lord Eldon seems to have been prepared to decide that each landowner had a right to insist upon every part of the works being constructed according to the parliamentary plan; but this doctrine has been modified in accordance with the judgment of Alderson, B., in *Lee* v. *Milner*:[8] "These Acts of Parliament have been

Lee v. *Milner*.

[8] 2 Y. & C. Exch. 611; 2 M. & W. 824; *Doe* v. *Bristol and*

called parliamentary bargains made with each of the landowners. Perhaps more correctly they ought to be treated as conditional powers given by Parliament to take the land of the different proprietors through whose estates the works are to proceed. Each landholder, therefore, has a right to have the powers strictly and literally carried into effect as regards his own land, and has a right also to require that no variation shall be made to his prejudice in the carrying into effect the bargain between the undertakers and any one else." "I cannot accede to the proposition that where the contract as far as regards the land of the complaining landowner is exactly performed, any variation made at a distant point, and with the consent of the landowner there, and producing no real injury to the complaining landowner, ought to be the ground for an injunction in a court of equity to be granted at his application."

Resources of company deficient. Right of Landowner to stop the works.

As a consequence of Lord Eldon's doctrine, it was held that if the resources of the promoters were clearly insufficient for the completion of the

Exeter Railway, 6 M. & W. 320; *York and North Midland Railway Company* v. *R.*, 1 E. & B. 858.

whole of the undertaking, any landowner was entitled to an injunction to prevent the compulsory powers from being exercised over his land.[9]

Mandamus to complete.

On the other hand, the Court of Queen's Bench decided that the Act of Parliament placed the promoters under an obligation to complete the works, which might be enforced by mandamus, and a deficiency of funds was apparently no answer to the writ.[1] Promoters might thus have been placed in a very awkward dilemma. It is now, however, settled that, as usually framed, the

Act permissive.

Act is permissive, and not obligatory, so that such a mandamus will not lie.[2] And in like

[9] *Agar* v. *Regent's Canal Company*, G. Coop. 77; *Mayor of King's Lynn* v. *Pemberton*, 1 Swanst. 244; *Blakemore* v. *Glamorganshire Canal Company*, 1 M. & K. 164; *Salmon* v. *Randall*, 3 M. & Cr. 439; *Attorney-General* v. *Birmingham Railway Company*, 3 Mac. & Gor. 453; *Gray* v. *Liverpool Railway Company*, 9 Beav. 391; *Hedges* v. *Metropolitan Railway Company*, 28 Beav. 109; see *Cohen* v. *Wilkinson*, 1 Mac. & Gor. 481; *Heathcote* v. *North Staffordshire Railway Company*, 2 Mac. & Gor. 100; *Graham* v. *Birkenhead, &c., Railway Company*, 2 Mac. & Gor. 146; *Hodgson* v. *Earl Powis*, 12 Beav. 529; *Logan* v. *Earl of Courtown*, 13 Beav. 22.

[1] *R.* v. *Eastern Counties Railway Company*, 10 A. & E. 531; *R.* v. *London and North Western Railway Company*, 16 Q. B. 864; *R.* v. *York, Newcastle, and Berwick Railway Company*, 16 Q. B. 886.

[2] *York and North Midland Railway Company* v. *R.*, 1 E. & B. 178, 858.

manner, upon the principle of *Lee* v. *Milner*, it would seem that the inability of the promoters to complete the undertaking does not of itself put them in default as regards a particular land-owner, so as to entitle him to say that his land shall not be taken. At all events, if the equitable doctrine remains, the facility with which additional capital can now be raised will render it difficult of application.

Agar v. *Regent's Canal Company.*

The first example of a suit to control the execution of a public work appears to be *Agar* v. *The Regent's Canal Company*,[3] where the bill was filed by the plaintiff as owner of an estate through which the defendants proposed to make the canal, which they were empowered to cut by a private Act of Parliament obtained by them for that purpose. The prayer of the bill sought an injunction to restrain the defendants from carrying the proposed canal through the plaintiff's garden and rickyard. An application was made upon the filing of the bill, supported by an affidavit of the facts, stated in the bill, for an injunction according to the prayer, and which the Lord Chancellor granted. Upon

[3] G. Coop. 77, 212, 221; 1 Swanst. 250.

the coming in of the answer the defendants moved to dissolve the above injunction, when it was varied so far as only to restrain the defendants from deviating in cutting their canal from the line prescribed by their Act of Parliament. The parties differing as to what was the prescribed line, the defendants proceeded to make the cut according to the judgment which they had formed on the matter. The plaintiff therefore moved to commit them for a breach of the injunction. Lord Eldon refused the motion as premature, saying that it must be first tried at law whether a trespass had been committed.

Interlocutory injunction.

The present practice is to grant an interlocutory injunction to protect the land until the question can be tried at law.[4] "I consider," said Lord Cottenham,[5] "that there cannot be a more useful exercise of the jurisdiction of this Court, than in interfering to ascertain the rights be-

[4] *Kemp* v. *London and Brighton Railway Company*, 1 Rlwy. Ca. 495; *Farrow* v. *Vansittart*, 1 Rlwy. Ca. 602; *Bell* v. *Hull and Selby Railway Company*, 1 Rlwy. Ca. 616; *Field* v. *Jackson*, Dick. 599; *Dudley* v. *Horton*, 4 L. J. Ch. 104; *Frewin* v. *Lewis*, 4 My. & Cr. 249.

[5] *Kemp* v. *London and Brighton Railway Company*, 1 Rlwy. Ca. 495.

tween parties circumstanced as in this case. I look at the great powers which are necessarily given to these companies; the variety of interests with which those powers may interfere, if not strictly exercised according to the provisions of the Acts; the necessity of immediate interposition; the injury to the parties, if there be not a jurisdiction constantly open, by which their respective rights may be ascertained: and then it appears to me that this is of all others a situation of things in which this Court ought to exercise that jurisdiction." "Now the course I have always adopted in cases where the question turns upon a legal right, is to put the parties in a situation to try as quickly as possible that legal right, and to protect the property to be affected until the legal right can be ascertained."

Injunction framed in general terms or specifically.

It rests in the discretion of the Court either to restrain an infringement of the plaintiff's rights in general terms, which was the course pursued in *Agar* v. *The Regent's Canal Company*, or else so to frame the order as to let the parties know what the Court considers their respective rights to be. The former plan is generally less convenient,

CHAP. IV.
Sect. 1.

but it may be adopted when an injunction is required before the question of right is ready for discussion.[6]

Sect. 2.

Sect. 2.—LANDS CLAUSES CONSOLIDATION ACT.[7]

(a.) *With respect to the Purchase of Lands by Agreement.*

Parties to sell and convey.
Clause 7.

By the 7th clause it is made lawful for tenants in tail,[8] and for life,[9] and for other persons having such limited interests as therein mentioned,[1] to sell and convey the fee simple.

Agreements before the passing of the Act.

The promoters of an undertaking frequently enter into agreements with the landowners, in

[6] *Cother* v. *Midland Railway Company*, 2 Phil. 469 ; 5 Rlwy. Ca. 187, 192 ; *Attorney-General* v. *London and South Western Railway Company*, 3 De G. & S. 439 ; 7 Rlwy. Ca. 624 ; *Dawson* v. *Paver*, 5 Hare, 430 ; *Broadbent* v. *Imperial Gas Company*, 7 D. M. G. 442 ; 7 H. L. C. 600.

[7] 8 & 9 Vict. c. 18. As to undertakings to which this Act may apply, although not expressly incorporated with the special Act, *Wale* v. *Westminster Palace Hotel Company*, 8 C. B. N. S. 276.

[8] The tenant of an inalienable estate tail with the reversion in the Crown, was held to be entitled to sell and convey the estate tail, but not the reversion, *Re Cuckfield Board*, 19 Beav. 153.

[9] As to tenancy for life with a proviso against alienation, *Devenish* v. *Brown*, 2 Jur. N. S. 1043. When the tenancy for life is equitable only, the trustees must join in the conveyance, *Lippincott* v. *Smyth*, 6 Jur. N. S. 311.

[1] *Douglass* v. *London and North Western Railway Company*, 3 K. & J. 173.

order to induce them to withdraw their opposition to the passing of the bill. Many instances have occurred of the company, when incorporated, refusing to perform such contracts. In a case of this sort[2] Lord Cottenham said, "The question is not whether there be any binding contract at law, but whether this Court will permit the company to use their powers under the Act in direct opposition to the arrangements made with the plaintiffs prior to the Act, upon the faith of which they were permitted to obtain such powers. If the company and the proprietors cannot be identified, still it is clear that the company have succeeded to, and are now in possession of, all that the proprietors had before; they are entitled to all their rights, and subject to all their liabilities. If any one had individually projected such a scheme, and in prosecution of it had entered into arrangements, and then had sold

Edwards v. Grand Junction Railway Company.

[2] *Edwards* v. *Grand Junction Railway Company*, 7 Sim. 337; 1 My. & Cr. 650; *Stanley* v. *Chester and Birkenhead Railway Company*, 9 Sim. 264; 3 My. & Cr. 773; *Lord Petre* v. *Eastern Counties Railway Company*, 1 Rlwy. Ca. 462. See also *Grenhalgh* v. *Manchester and Birmingham Railway Company*, 3 My. & Cr. 784; *Vauxhall Bridge Company* v. *Earl Spencer*, Jac. 64; Fry on Specific Performance, 61.

CHAP. IV. Sect. 2.

and assigned all his interest in it to another, there would be no legal obligation between those who had dealt with the original projector and such a purchaser; but in this court it would be otherwise. So here, as the company stand in the place of the projectors, they cannot repudiate arrangements into which such projectors had entered; they cannot exercise the powers given by Parliament to such projectors, in their corporate capacity, and at the same time refuse to comply with those terms, upon the faith of which all opposition to their obtaining such powers was withheld."

Qualifications of Lord Cottenham's doctrine.

It is settled by two decisions[3] of the House of Lords that this doctrine does not apply, unless (1.) The company has taken the benefit of the agreement; (2.) The agreement is for something warranted by the terms of the incorporation.

[3] *Preston* v. *Liverpool, Manchester, and Newcastle Railway Company*, 5 H. L. C. 605; 1 Sim. N. S. 586; 17 Beav. 114; see *Earl of Lindsey* v. *Great Northern Railway Company*, 10 Hare, 664; *Gooday* v. *Colchester, &c., Railway Company*, 17 Beav. 132; *Williams* v. *St. George's Harbour Company*, 24 Beav. 339; 2 D. F. & J. 547. *Caledonian Railway Company* v. *St. Helensburgh*, 2 Macq. 391; see *Leominster Canal Company* v. *Shrewsbury and Hereford Railway Company*, 3 K. & J. 654.

Sect. 2. Disapproval.

Moreover, in considering these cases, Lords Cranworth and Brougham expressed a strong disapproval of the whole doctrine, upon the ground that the Act, when passed, becomes the charter of the company, prescribing its duties and declaring its rights, so that all persons becoming shareholders have a right to consider that they are entitled to all the benefits held out to them by the Act, and liable to no obligations beyond those which are there indicated.

Existing company applying for power to make further works.

It is, however, settled, that an existing company applying to Parliament for powers to make further works, may enter into a valid contract with a landowner for the purchase of any part of his land on which they propose to construct their works.[4]

Contracts conditional.

Such contracts will in general be construed to be conditional on the Act passing, and perhaps also on the land specified being required. It may be doubted whether the directors would

[4] *Hawkes* v. *Eastern Counties Railway Company,* 3 De G. & S. 743 ; 1 D. M. G. 737 ; 5 H. L. C. 331. A query was thrown out in this case whether the directors of a company could accept a defective title.

CHAP. IV. Sect. 2.

have power to bind the shareholders in such a contract absolutely.[5]

(b.) *With respect to the Purchase and Taking of Lands otherwise than by Agreement.*

Notice to treat.

When the promoters shall require to purchase or take[6] any lands which they are authorised to purchase or take, they shall give notice to the parties[7] interested therein, or enabled by the Act to sell and convey the same. The notice usually describes the property by reference to the deposited plans. It should, of course, be accurately drawn.[8]

Clause 18.

Second notice.

The promoters are not bound to comprise the whole of the land which they may require in the

[5] *Webb* v. *Direct London and Portsmouth Railway Company*, 1 D. M. G. 521; *Lord James Stuart* v. *London and North Western Railway Company*, 1 D. M. G. 721; *Gage* v. *Newmarket Railway Company*, 18 Q. B. 457; *Edinburgh, Perth, and Dundee Railway Company* v. *Philip*, 2 Macq. 514; *Scottish North Eastern Railway Company* v. *Stewart*, 3 Macq. 382; Fry on Specific Performance, p. 287.

[6] The word "take" refers to clauses 58 to 67. See 9 Hare, 445.

[7] It is not necessary to serve the owner of a mere easement, as a wayleave over the property; *Thicknesse* v. *Lancaster Canal Company*, 4 M. & W. 484.

[8] See Form, Hodges' Law of Railways, App. 231; *Kemp* v. *London and Brighton Railway Company*, 1 Rlwy. Ca. 495.

first notice, but they may from time to time, until their powers expire, serve fresh notices for taking any additional land which may be requisite for the works;[9] but after once giving a notice, they cannot withdraw it and give a second notice for taking less,[1] nor can they abandon it altogether, even on the ground of a deficiency of funds.[2]

Receding from a notice.

But where the Commissioners of Woods were authorised to lay out 200,000*l.* in the formation of Battersea Park, and they served notices to treat in order to ascertain the expense of carrying out a particular plan, the claims sent in proving to be largely in excess of the funds available, it was held that the commissioners might recede from the notices.[3] And it appears that promoters

[9] *Stamps* v. *Birmingham, Wolverhampton and Stour Valley Railway Company*, 7 Hare, 251 ; 6 Rlwy. Ca. 123 ; *Simpson* v. *Lancaster and Carlisle Railway Company*, 15 Sim. 580 ; *Webb* v. *Manchester and Leeds Railway Company*, 4 My. & Cr. 116 ; *Williams* v. *South Wales Railway Company*, 3 De G. & S. 354 ; *Sadd* v. *Maldon, Witham, and Braintree Railway Company*, 6 Exch. 143.

[1] *Tawney* v. *Lynn and Ely Railway Company*, 4 Rlwy. Ca. 615 ; 16 L. J. Ch. 282.

[2] *R.* v. *Commissioners of Manchester*, 4 B. & Ad. 333 ; *R.* v. *Hungerford Market Company*, 4 B. & Ad. 327.

[3] *R.* v. *Commissioners of Woods*, 15 Q. B. 761 ; see 8 & 9 Vict. c. 38.

CHAP. IV. Sect. 2.

who have given notice to take part of a property, and are then required, under the 92nd section, to take the whole, may withdraw their notice and refuse to take any part.[4]

Liberty to make a tunnel.

A question has been raised, whether promoters wishing to make a tunnel under lands, or to throw an arch over them, can compel the landowner to sell them the liberty of doing so, or whether they are under the necessity of purchasing the entire close.[5]

Specific performance.

There has been much difference of opinion whether, after the service of a notice, the landowner and the company are brought within the ordinary jurisdiction of the Court as to the specific performance of contracts.[6]

Waiver of notice.

Where a landowner had waived the service of a notice, he was not allowed to take an objection for the waut of it.[7]

[4] *R.* v. *London and South Western Railway Company*, 12 Q. B. 775; 5 Rlwy. Ca. 669; *King* v. *Wycombe Railway Company*, 28 Beav. 104; see further as to 92nd sect. post, p. 230.

[5] *Pinchin* v. *London and Blackwall Railway Company*, 1 K. & J. 34; 5 D. M. G. 851; see *Sparrow* v. *Oxford, Worcester, and Wolverhampton Railway Company*, 2 D. M. G. 108.

[6] The cases are collected in *Haynes* v. *Haynes*, 1 Dr. & Sm. 426.

[7] *R.* v. *South Holland*, 8 A. & E. 429.

CHAP. IV.
Sect. 2.
Compensation.
Clause 21 *et seq.*

The Act then provides for the manner in which, in case of dispute, compensation shall be settled for the interest in lands which the party is enabled to sell, or for any damage that may be sustained by him by reason of the execution of the works.

Clause 63.
Severance.

In estimating such compensation, regard is to be had not only to the value of the land to be purchased or taken, but also to the damage, if any, to be sustained by the owner by reason of the severing[8] of the lands taken from the other lands of such owner, or otherwise injuriously affecting such other lands by the exercise of the parliamentary powers.

Clause 68.

Moreover, the 68th section provides that, if any party shall be entitled to any compensation in respect of any lands, or of any interest therein, which shall have been taken for, or injuriously affected by, the execution of the works, and for which the promoters of the undertaking shall not have made satisfaction, such compensa-

[8] *South Wales Railway Company* v. *Richards*, 18 L. J. Q. B. 310; *Manning* v. *Eastern Counties Railway Company*, 12 M. & W. 237; *Grand Junction Railway Company* v. *White*, 2 Rlwy. Ca. 559; in *Re Duke of Beaufort*, 6 Jur. N. S. 979.

Chap. IV. Sect. 2.

tion shall be assessed in manner therein mentioned.[9]

Assessment of purchase-money.

The general rule is to assess the purchase-money according to the value of the land at the time of the notice: but under a particular Act, the assessment was made according to the value of the land at the time of passing the Act.[1]

Site of a church.

Where a company took the site of a church under their powers, the purchase-money was assessed on the footing of the commercial value of the land, and not according to the return which the church made in pew-rents, &c., when dedicated to spiritual purposes.[2]

Subjacent minerals.

The right to compensation in respect of subjacent minerals has been already discussed.[3]

Lands injuriously affected.

With respect to the compensation payable for lands which are injuriously affected, but not taken, the law is now settled in accordance with

[9] This clause refers to the entry and user spoken of in clause 85, and to land injuriously affected where no adjoining lands of the same owner have been taken; *Doe* v. *North Staffordshire Railway Company*, 20 L. J. Q. B. 249; *Burkenshaw* v. *Birmingham and Oxford Junction Railway Company*, 5 Exch. 475; *Perks* v. *Wycombe Railway Company*, 10 W. R. 788. See, as to Waterworks Act, *Ferrand* v. *Bradford*, 21 Beav. 412.

[1] *Manning* v. *Commissioners West India Dock Act*, 9 East. 165.

[2] *Hilcoats* v. *Archbishop of Canterbury*, 10 C. B. 327.

[3] Ante, p. 158.

the opinion of the learned judges who advised the Lord Chancellor in *Broadbent* v. *The Imperial Gas Company*[4] (that is to say):

Broadbent v. Imperial Gas Works.

"The cases relating to railways seem to us to establish, that compensation is given in respect of the calculable damage caused or to be caused in or by the execution of the permanent works of the company authorised by statute—for instance, obstructing ways or injuring lights—(as to when future damage may be assessed, see the judgment of Baron Parke in *Lee* v. *Milner*[5]); that an injurious act, unauthorised by statute, or done by the company negligently in abuse of their statutory powers, is the proper subject of an action; and that any act other than the erection of the permanent works, if properly done by the company in pursuance of the statute, whatever damage it may cause, is considered sufficiently compensated for by the public benefit expected to follow, and is neither a subject of action nor of compensation."

[4] 7 D. M. G. 459; 7 H. L. C. 600; *Glover* v. *North Staffordshire Railway Company*, 16 Q. B. 912; *Ware* v. *Regent's Canal Company*, 3 D. & J. 227; *Caledonian Railway Company* v. *Colt*, 3 Macq. 833.

[5] 2 M. & W. 824, post, p. 226.

CHAP. IV.
Sect. 2
Cases in which compensation clauses apply.

There is authority to the effect that the compensation clauses apply under the following circumstances:

For injury to the access to property, as by obstructing a private road,[6] or altering a public road on which the claimant's land abuts.[7]

For obstructing the access to a ferry.[8]

For obstructing the flow of water to a mill[9] or tanyard.[1]

For drowning a mine by the diversion of a brook.[2]

For causing drainage water to flow on to the premises.[3]

[6] *Glover* v. *North Staffordshire Railway Company*, 16 Q. B. 912; *Thicknesse* v. *Lancaster Canal Company*, 4 M. & W. 472; *South Staffordshire Railway Company* v. *Hall*, 3 Mac. & Gor. 353.

[7] *R.* v. *Eastern Counties Railway Company*, 2 Q. B. 347; 2 Rlwy. Ca. 736; *Phillips* v. *London and Brighton Railway Company*, V.-C. S., July, 1862; *Moore* v. *Great Southern and Western Railway Company*, 10 Ir. C. L. 46; *Tuohey* v. *Great Southern and Western Railway Company*, 10 Ir. C. L. 98.

[8] *R.* v. *Great Northern Railway Company*, 14 Q. B. 25.

[9] *R.* v. *Nottingham Old Water Works*, 6 A. & E. 355.

[1] *Mortimer* v. *South Wales Railway Company*, 5 Jur. N. S. 784.

[2] *R.* v. *North Midland Railway Company*, 2 Rlwy. Ca. 1; see *Bagnall* v. *London and North Western Railway Company*, 10 W. R. 232.

[3] *R.* v. *North Union Railway Company*, 1 Rlwy. Ca. 729.

For obstructing the access of light and air, and perhaps for causing dust and dirt to drift on to the claimant's premises.[4]

For loss of tolls to the owner of a towing path by reason of a diversion of the river.[5]

For damage caused by vibration during the construction of the works.[6]

Cases in which the compensation clauses do not apply.

The following are instances in which the compensation clauses seem not to be applicable:

For crossing a highway by a railroad on a level,[7]

[4] *Duke of Norfolk* v. *Tennant*, 16 Jur. 398; *Beardmer* v. *London and North Western Railway Company*, 1 Mac. & Gor. 112; *East and West India Docks* v. *Gattke*, 3 Mac. & Gor. 155; see *Turner* v. *Sheffield and Rotherham Company*, 10 M. & W. 425.

[5] *Rex* v. *Commissioners of Thames and Isis Navigation*, 5 A. & E. 804. This is a very doubtful authority; see 2 Rlwy. Ca. 748.

[6] *Penny* v. *South Eastern Railway Company*, 7 E. & B. 660.

[7] *Caledonian Railway Company* v. *Ogilvy*, 2 Macq. 229; *R.* v. *London Dock Company*, 5 A. & E. 163; *London and North Western Railway Company* v. *Smith*, 1 Mac. & Gor. 216; *East and West Indian Dock Company* v. *Gattke*, 3 Mac. & Gor. 155; *Wilkes* v. *Hungerford Market Company* 2 Bing. N. C. 281. But see *Chamberlaine* v. *West End and Crystal Palace Railway Company*, 10 W. R. 645. Where a railroad passed under a public road by a tunnel the company had to make compensation to the owner of the soil. *Ramsden* v. *Manchester, &c., Railway Company*, 1 Exch. 723. See *Board of Works for Wandsworth* v. *London and South Western Railway Company*, V.-C. K. 10 W. R. 814.

CHAP. IV. Sect. 2.

frightening horses on the highway,[8] or polluting a navigable river,[9] although the inconvenience to the claimant may amount to such special damage as would support an action.

For the loss of tithes on the land taken for the works,[1] unless the tithe owner is protected by the special Act.[2]

For intercepting the percolation of water to a well.[3]

For loss of privacy, by reason of the premises being overlooked by passengers on a railway.[4]

For vibration caused by the passage of trains, after a railway is opened for traffic.[5]

How compensation is to be assessed.

Generally speaking, compensation is to be assessed once for all, for the injury authorised to be caused to the rights of the landowners; and if any extraordinary unforeseen damage occurs,

[8] *Rex* v. *Pease*, 4 B. & Ad. 30; see 8 & 9 Vict. c. 20, s. 63.

[9] *R.* v. *Bristol Dock Company*, 12 East, 429; see *Sutton Harbour Company* v. *Hitchens*, 13 Beav. 408; 1 D. M. G. 161; *Abraham* v. *Great Northern Railway Company*, 15 Jur. 855.

[1] *Rex* v. *Commissioners of Nene Outfall*, 9 B. & C. 875.

[2] *London and Blackwall Railway Company* v. *Letts*, 5 Hare, 605; 3 H. L. C. 470; see 7 & 8 Vict. c. 85, s. 22.

[3] *New River Company* v. *Johnson*, 6 Jur. N. S. 374.

[4] *Penny* v. *South Eastern Railway Company*, 7 E. & B. 660.

[5] *Penny* v. *South Eastern Railway Company*, 7 E. & B. 660; see *London and North Western Railway Company* v. *Bradley*, 3 Mac. & Gor. 336.

CHAP. IV. Sect. 2.

the suffering party is without remedy.[6] But promoters are liable to an action for negligence in the construction, or maintenance of the works, or in the general management of the undertaking.[7]

Actions against promoters.

In one case Lord Cottenham restrained a landowner from having compensation assessed according to the Act, on the ground that the promoters disputed their liability to pay any;[8] but this decision has been clearly overruled.[9]

Restraining a landowner.

[6] *Caledonian Railway Company* v. *Lockhart*, 3 Macq. 808; *Little* v. *Dublin and Drogheda Railway Company*, 7 Ir. C. L. 82; see *Lee* v. *Milner*, 2 M. & W. 824.

[7] *Lawrence* v. *Great Northern Railway Company*, 16 Q. B., 643; *Bagnall* v. *London and North Western Railway Company*, 7 H. & N. 423, 452; 10 W. R. 802; *Bruce* v. *Great Western Railway Company*, 31 L. J. Q. B. 101; *Clothier* v. *Webster*, 31 L. J. C. P. 316; *Vaughan* v. *Taff Vale Railway Company*, 5 H. & N. 679; *Whitehouse* v. *Birmingham Canal Company*, 27 L. J. Exch. 25; *Witherley* v. *Regent's Canal Company*, 12 C. B. N. S. 2; *Cockburn* v. *Erewash Company*, Q. B. As to the liability of public commissioners or trustees, see *Gibbs* v. *Trustees of Liverpool Docks*, 1 H. & N. 439; 3 H. & N. 164; *Mersey Dock Board* v. *Penhallow*, 7 H. & N. 329.

[8] *London and North Western Railway Company* v. *Smith*, 1 Mac. & Gor. 216.

[9] *East and West India Dock Company* v. *Gattke*, 3 Mac. & Gor. 155; *London and North Western Railway Company* v. *Bradley*, 3 Mac. & Gor. 336; *South Staffordshire Railway Company* v. *Hall*, 3 Mac. & Gor. 353; *Lancashire and Yorkshire Railway Company* v. *Evans*, 15 Beav. 322; *Sutton Harbour Company* v. *Hitchens*, 13 Beav. 408; 1 D. M. G. 161; *Caledonian Railway Company* v. *Ogilvy*, 2 Macq. 229; see *Duke of Norfolk* v. *Tenant*, 16 Jur. 398; *R.* v. *Lancaster and Preston Junction*

CHAP. IV.

Sect. 2.
Entry.
Clauses 84 & 85.

(c.) *Miscellaneous.*

It is provided that if the promoters shall be desirous of entering[1] upon and using any lands before the amount to be paid has been determined, they shall first deposit[2] in the bank the sum claimed by any party who shall not consent, or such sum as a surveyor[3] appointed by two justices shall determine, and give a bond with two sureties to be approved[4] by two justices in a penal sum equal to the deposit, conditioned[5] for

Railway Company, 6 Q. B. 759; *R.* v. *London and North Western Railway Company*, 3 E. & B. 443; *Re Bradby*, 4 E. & B. 1014; *Re Byles*, 11 Exch. 464.

[1] As to entry for the purpose of surveying, *Fooks* v. *Wilts, Somerset, and Weymouth Railway Company*, 4 Rlwy. Ca. 210.

[2] As to deposit before valuation, *Stamps* v. *Birmingham, &c., Railway Company*, 6 Rlwy. Ca. 126.

[3] Query if he may be the company's surveyor, *Langham* v. *Great Northern Railway*, 1 De G. & S. 486; *Barker* v. *North Staffordshire Railway Company*, 2 De G. & S. 55.

[4] Sureties may be appointed without notice to the landowner, *Bridges* v. *Wilts and Somerset Railway Company*, 4 Rlwy. Ca. 622; *Langham* v. *Great Northern Railway Company*, 1 De G. & S. 486; *Poynder* v. *Great Northern Railway Company*, 16 Sim. 3; 2 Phil. 330.

[5] The condition of the bond should adopt the language of the section, *Hoskins* v. *Phillips*, 3 Exch. 181; *Poynder* v. *Great Northern Railway Company*, 16 Sim. 3; 2 Phil. 330; *Barker* v. *North Staffordshire Railway Company*, 2 De G. & S. 55; *Dakin* v. *London and North Western Railway Company*, 3 De G. & S. 414; *Willey* v. *South Eastern Railway Company*, 1 Mac. & Gor. 58.

payment to such party,[6] or for deposit in the bank for the benefit of the parties interested in such lands as the case may require, of the purchase money or compensation.[7]

The foregoing sections apply only to lands taken, and not to lands injuriously affected.[8]

Promoters taking possession on agreement with the tenants only.

The promoters sometimes take possession of the land after settling with the tenants only. This is an erroneous course.[9] In such a case an order was made at the suit of the reversioner that the promoters should lodge money and give

[6] A bond conditioned for payment to landowners jointly, when they were tenants in common, held to be bad, *Langham* v. *Great Northern Railway Company*, 1 De G. & S. 486.

[7] Other cases in which the lawfulness of the entry of the promoters has been questioned are, *Doe* v. *Manchester, &c., Railway*, 14 M. & W. 687 ; *Doe* d. *Hudson* v. *Leeds and Bradford Railway Company*, 15 Jur. 946 ; *Standish* v. *Mayor of Liverpool*, 1 Dr. 1 ; *Newton* v. *Metropolitan Railway Company*, 10 W. R. 102 ; *Jones* v. *Great Western Railway Company*, 1 Rlwy. Ca. 684 ; *Langford* v. *Brighton and Lewes Railway Company*, 4 Rlwy. Ca. 69 ; *Skerratt* v. *North Staffordshire Railway Company*, 5 Rlwy. Ca. 166 ; *South Western Railway Company* v. *Coward*, 5 Rlwy. Ca. 703. Taking a stream under Waterworks Clauses Act, *Ferrand* v. *Corporation of Bradford*, 21 Beav. 412.

[8] *Hutton* v. *London and South Western Railway Company*, 7 Hare, 262 ; *Lister* v. *Lobley*, 7 A. & E. 124 ; *Innocent* v. *North Midland Railway Company*, 1 Rlwy. Ca. 242.

[9] *Inge* v. *Birmingham, Wolverhampton, and Stour Valley Company*, 3 D. M. G. 666 ; *Alston* v. *Eastern Counties Railway Company*, 1 Jur. N. S. 1009 ; *Carnochan* v. *Norwich and Spalding Railway Company*, 26 Beav. 169.

CHAP. IV.
Sect. 2.

a bond according to the 85th section, or else an injunction was to go to restrain them from proceeding with the works.[1] But where the reversioner disputed the right of the promoters to take the land, Shadwell, V.-C., refused to restrain them from summoning a jury to assess its value, on the ground that, if the plaintiff was right, such proceeding would be a nullity. And he also refused to restrain the company from raising an embankment on the land.[2]

Taking part of a house or manufactory.
Clause 92.

By the 92nd section it is enacted, "That no party shall at any time be required to sell or convey to the promoters of the undertaking a part only of any house or other building or manufactory, if such party be willing and able to sell and convey the whole thereof."

The construction of the word "house" has been settled by authority to mean all that would pass under the grant of a house in a conveyance, and therefore to include the curtilage and garden.[3]

There is more difficulty as to the meaning of

[1] *Armstrong* v. *Waterford and Limerick Railway Company*, 10 Ir. Eq. 60.

[2] *Mouchet* v. *Great Western Railway Company*, 1 Rlwy. Ca. 567.

[3] *Lord Robert Grosvenor* v. *Hampstead Junction Railway Company*, 1 D. & J. 446 ; *St. Thomas's Hospital* v. *Charing Cross*

the word "manufactory." In *Barker* v. *North Staffordshire Railway Company*,[4] two brine pits were considered to be part of certain salt works within the meaning of the Act; and in *Sparrow* v. *Oxford, Worcester, and Wolverhampton Railway Company*,[5] land included in the same wall with tin-plate works, but separated from them by a road, and used for the deposit of ashes from the works, was held to be part of the manufactory. The works had been built after the passing of the Act. In another case, cottages used as warehouses in connection with a manufactory situate on the opposite side of a public road, were held to be part of the manufactory.[6]

However, in *Reddin* v. *The Metropolitan Board of Works*,[7] where the plaintiff carried on the

Railway Company, 1 J. & H. 400; *Cole* v. *West End and Crystal Palace Railway Company*, 27 Beav. 242; *Alexander* v. *West End and Crystal Palace Railway Company*, 8 Jur. N. S. 833; *King* v. *Wycombe Railway Company*, 28 Beav. 104; *Hewson* v. *London and South Western Railway Company*, 8 W. R. 467. A statutory owner is able to sell and convey within the meaning of this section, 1 J. & H. 406.

[4] 2 De G. & S. 55.

[5] 9 Hare, 436; 2 D. M. G. 94.

[6] *Spackman* v. *The Great Western Railway Company*, 1 Jur. N. S. 790.

[7] 10 W. R. 726, 764. See also *R.* v. *London and Greenwich Railway Company*, 2 Gale & D. 444.

CHAP. IV.
Sect. 2.

business of a dust contractor, which consists in collecting and sorting dust heaps, and also, as a subsidiary business, worked up some of the components into plaster-powder and manure, the promoters having served a notice to take a "totshop," which was used only in connection with the sorting process, it was held that they could not be compelled to take the whole of the premises.

Counter notice and entry.

It has been held that where the promoters are met by a counter notice under this section, they cannot enter upon the land comprised in their own notice without giving security for the value of the whole;[8] and a landowner was allowed to avail himself of this section, after negotiating with the company to fix the price of the land comprised in their notice.[9] Where the original notice was for the purchase of the easement of throwing an arch over a yard, and it was met by a counter notice to take the whole manufactory, it was held that, whether the original notice was

[8] *Giles* v. *London, Chatham, and Dover Railway Company*, 1 Dr. & S. 406; *Dadson* v. *East Kent Railway Company* and *Underwood* v. *Bedford and Cambridge Railway Company*, 7 Jur. N. S. 941; *Barker* v. *North Staffordshire Railway Company*, 2 De G. & S. 55.

[9] *Gardner* v. *Charing Cross Railway Company*, 10 W. R. 120; *Hedges* v. *Metropolitan Railway Company*, 28 Beav. 109.

good or not, the promoters would not be restrained from entering upon and purchasing the whole after the compulsory powers had expired.[1]

CHAP. IV. Sect. 2.

Intersected land. Clause 94.

The expression "such land" in the 94th section is not restricted to intersected lands situate in a town, but applies to all intersected lands, whether so situate or not.[2]

Mortgagees. Clause 108 *et seq.*

The promoters must satisfy mortgagees of the land before taking possession.[3]

Lessees.

The clauses from 119 to 122 deal with lands subject to leases, and amongst other things, they provide that where part only of the lands in lease are required, the lessee shall be entitled to receive from the promoters compensation for the damage done to him in his tenancy by severance or otherwise, by reason of the execution of the works.

Compensation.

In some cases under the Hungerford Market Act,[4] lessees appear to have been held entitled to

[1] *Pinchin* v. *London and Blackwall Railway Company*, 1 K. & J. 69; 5 D. M. G. 851; and see *ante*, p. 220.

[2] *Eastern Counties Railway Company* v. *Marriage*, 2 H. & N. 625; 9 H. L. C. 32.

[3] *Rankin* v. *East and West India Docks Company*, 12 Beav. 298. See *Mold* v. *Wheatcroft*, 27 Beav. 510.

[4] *Ex parte Farlow*, 2 B. & Ad. 341; *R.* v. *Hungerford Market Company*, 4 B. & Ad. 592; *Re Palmer*, 9 A. & E. 463; *R.* v. *Hungerford Market Company*, 4 B. & Ad. 596.

Chap. IV. Sect. 2.

compensation for the loss of their chance of renewal, but this is not the general rule.[5] A tradesman is not entitled to compensation for a loss of business consequent only upon other houses in the neighbourhood being taken down;[6] but if he is obliged to leave his own premises he may recover for the loss sustained in removing.[7]

Tenant from year to year.

The compensation payable to a tenant from year to year is to be determined by two justices, and not by arbitration.[8] He appears to be liable for the apportioned rent up to the time when the land is taken from him.[9] A tenant from year to year on a Christmas tenancy received six months' notice to quit on the 10th January, and the company applied for possession at Michaelmas. The tenant refused to go out, and they did not take any steps to compel him until the following Christmas. It was held that he was not entitled to compensation.[1]

[5] *R.* v. *Liverpool and Manchester Railway Company*, 4 A. & E. 650.

[6] *R.* v. *London Dock Company*, 5 A. & E. 163.

[7] *Jubb* v. *Hull Dock Company*, 9 Q. B. 443.

[8] *Ex parte Nadin*, 17 L. J. Ch. 421; *R.* v. *Manchester, Sheffield, and Lincolnshire Railway Company*, 4 E. & B. 88.

[9] *Wainwright* v. *Ramsden*, 5 M. & W. 602; 1 Rlwy. Ca. 714.

[1] *R.* v. *Southampton Railway Company*, 10 A. & E. 3; 2 Per. & D. 243; 1 Rlwy. Ca. 717.

In *Doo* v. *Landon and Croydon Railway Company*,[2] the plaintiff held a lease from a canal company of a wharf and premises for twenty-one years, determinable by the canal company on certain terms, after six months' notice. The defendants applied to Parliament for power to purchase the canal, and entered into an agreement with the plaintiff, and other lessees, to buy off their opposition to the bill. They were not allowed, after obtaining the Act, to determine the lease on notice.

Expiration of powers. Clause 123.

Unless otherwise prescribed in the special Act, the powers for the compulsory purchase or taking of lands, shall not be exercised after the expiration of three years from the passing of the special Act.

Notice served before expiration.

It is now settled that if the notice is served before the expiration of the period prescribed for the exercise of the compulsory powers, the promoters may proceed to complete their title after that period;[3] and mere delay on their part after

[2] 1 Rlwy. Ca. 257.

[3] *Sparrow* v. *Oxford, Worcester, and Wolverhampton Railway Company*, 9 Hare, 436; 2 D. M. G. 94; *Brocklebank* v. *Whitehaven Junction Railway Company*, 15 Sim. 632; *Kinnersley* v. *North Staffordshire Railway Company*, 6 Rlwy. Ca. 662; *Mar-*

CHAP. IV. Sect. 2.

the service of the notice does not raise any equity, because the landowner has a remedy by mandamus.[4] Where a company had given notice to take part of a manufactory, a few days before the time fixed for the expiration of their compulsory powers, and a counter notice to take the whole was duly served upon them after that time, the Court would not restrain them from completing the purchase under the Act.[5]

Clause 124.

Provision is made for the purchase at any time by the promoters of interests in land, the purchase of which has been omitted by mistake.[6]

quis of Salisbury v. *Great Northern Railway Company*, 7 Rlwy. Ca. 175; *R.* v. *Birmingham and Oxford Junction Railway Company*, 19 L. J. Q. B. 453; 15 Q. B. 634; see *River Dun Navigation Company* v. *North Midland Railway Company*, 1 Rlwy. Ca. 135; *R.* v. *Oxford and Birmingham Railway Company*, 14 Jur. 899; *Doe* v. *Bristol and Exeter Railway Company*, 6 M. & W. 320; 2 Rlwy. Ca. 75; *Seymour* v. *London and South Western Railway Company*, 5 Jur. N. S. 753.

[4] *Sparrow* v. *Oxford, Worcester, and Wolverhampton Railway Company*, 9 Hare, 436; 2 D. M. G. 94; *Pinchin* v. *London and Blackwall Railway Company*, 1 K. & J. 69; 5 D. M. G. 851; see *Hedges* v. *Metropolitan Railway Company*, 28 Beav. 109.

[5] *Pinchin* v. *London and Blackwall Railway Company*, 1 K. & J. 34; 5 D. M. G. 851; see *Schwinge* v. *London and Blackwall Railway Company*, 3 S. & G. 30.

[6] *Meynell* v. *Surtees*, 1 Jur. N. S. 80; *Alston* v. *Eastern Counties Railway Company*, 1 Jur. N. S. 1009; *Duke of Beaufort* v. *Patrick*, 22 L. J. Ch. 489; *Somersetshire Coal Canal Company* v. *Harcourt*, 24 Beav. 571; on appeal, 2 D. & J. 596;

Where lands are in the possession of a receiver of the court, the promoters should apply for leave before taking proceedings under the Act.[7]

CHAP. IV. Sect. 2. Receiver.

Sect. 3.—CONSTRUCTION OF A RAILWAY.

Sect. 3.

(a.) *Special Act.*

In pursuance of the Standing Orders, plans of the projected railway and of the lands which the company may require to take or use, with a book of reference containing the names of the owners, lessees, and occupiers of such lands, have to be deposited with the clerks of the peace of the respective counties.[8]

Plans.

The special Act usually enacts to the effect that it shall be lawful[9] for the company to make

General powers.

Mold v. *Wheatcroft*, 27 Beav. 510 ; *Doe* v. *Manchester*, 12 C. B. 474, 5 De G. & S. 249 ; *Marquis of Salisbury* v. *Great Northern Railway Company*, 5 C. B. N. S. 174 ; *Jolly* v. *Great Northern Railway Company*, 8 Jur. N. S. 1019.

[7] *Tink* v. *Rundle*, 10 Beav. 318 ; *Richards* v. *Richards*, J. 255.

[8] A landowner is not in general expected to examine the plans deposited in a neighbouring county, *Bentinck* v. *Norfolk Estuary Company*, 26 L. J. Ch. 404 ; 3 Jur. N. S. 204.

[9] These words are permissive only so that a mandamus will not lie to compel the company to construct the line, *York and North Midland Railway Company* v. *R.*, 1 E. & B. 178, 858 ; *Great Western Railway Company* v. *R.*, 1 E. & B. 874 ; *R.* v. *Lancashire and Yorkshire Railway Company*, 1 E. & B. 228 ;

CHAP. IV. Sect. 3.

and maintain the railway and works in the line,[1] and upon the lands[2] delineated in the plans and described in the books of reference, and to enter upon and take and use[3] such of the

Scottish North Eastern Railway Company v. *Stewart*, 3 Macq. 382; *Warden and Assistants of Dover Harbour* v. *London, Chatham, and Dover Railway Company*, 7 Jur. N. S. 453; *Edinburgh, Perth, and Dundee Railway Company* v. *Philip*, 2 Macq. 514; *Nicholl* v. *Allen*, 1 B. & S. 916.

[1] That is, in the datum line, subject to the powers of deviation given by the general Act. *The North British Railway Company* v. *Tod*, 12 Cl. & F. 722; *Breynton* v. *London and North Western Railway Company*, 2 C. P. Coop. 108; *R.* v. *Caledonian Railway Company*, 16 Q. B. 19; *Beardmer* v. *London and North Western Railway Company*, 1 Mac. & Gor. 112; *Ware* v. *Regent's Canal Company*, 3 D. & J. 212; see *Feoffees of Heriot's Hospital*, 2 Dow. 301; *Squire* v. *Campbell*, 1 My. & Cr. 459; *Mott* v. *Blackwall Railway Company*, 2 Phil. 632; *Aldred* v. *North Midland Railway Company*, 1 Rlwy. Ca. 404. The plans deposited are not binding further upon the company. For provisions in earlier Acts, see *Doe* v. *Bristol and Exeter Railway Company*, 6 M. & W. 320; *Doe* v. *North Staffordshire Railway Company*, 20 L. J. Q. B. 249.

[2] In *Manchester, Sheffield, and Lincolnshire Railway Company* v. *Great Northern Railway Company*, 9 Hare, 284, two Acts of Parliament conferred on different companies the power of purchasing compulsorily the same plot of land.

[3] A canal company was authorised to take lands "to and for the use of the navigation, but to or for no other use or purpose whatsoever." It was held (*dubitante* Erle), that they could not lawfully let out boats for hire on a reservoir formed in part upon land taken under the powers of the Act from the estate of an ancestor of the plaintiff. The plaintiff had a right of fishing and fowling on the reservoir. *Bostock* v. *North Staffordshire Railway Company*, 4 E. & B. 798; 5 De G. & S. 584, and 2 Jur. N. S. 249, V.-C. S. A landowner has no equity to have his land

said lands as shall be necessary[4] for such purpose.

Land not required for the purposes of the Act.

Of course the company will not be allowed to take any land, even although it is delineated and described in the plans and book of reference, unless it is required *bonâ fide* for an authorised purpose.[5]

Junctions.

Questions have arisen upon the construction of certain special Acts as to the extent to which a new company could exercise their compulsory powers over land already vested in an earlier

reconveyed, if the line is abandoned, beyond what is given by the 127th and 128th sections of the general Act, *Astley* v. *Manchester, Sheffield, and Lincolnshire Railway Company*, 2 D. & J. 453.

[4] This means necessary for the stations and other conveniences, as well as for the actual line. *Cother* v. *Midland Railway Company*, 5 Rlwy. Ca. 187; 2 Phil. 469; *Crawfurd* v. *Chester and Holyhead Railway Company*, 11 Jur. 917; *Richards* v. *Scarborough Public Market Company*, 23 L. J. Ch. 110; *Re Dylar's Estate*, 1 Jur. N. S. 975; *Midland Railway Company* v. *Ambergate, &c., Railway Company*, 10 Hare, 359; *Sadd* v. *Maldon, Witham, and Braintree Railway Company*, 6 Ex. 143. The words stations and conveniences are now often inserted in the Act.

[5] *Webb* v. *Manchester and Leeds Railway Company*, 4 My. & Cr. 116; *Eversfield* v. *Mid-Sussex Railway*, 1 Giff. 153; 3 D. J. 286; *Bentinck* v. *Norfolk Estuary Company*, 26 L. J. Ch. 404; 3 Jur. N. S. 204; *Stockton and Darlington Railway Company* v. *Brown*, 9 H. L. C. 246; *Wood* v. *Epsom and Leatherhead Railway Company*, 8 C. B. N. S. 731; *Dodd* v. *Salisbury and Yeovil Railway Company*, 1 Giff. 158.

Chap. IV. Sect. 3.

company, with whose line they proposed to make a junction.[5]

Special clauses.

Landowners who wish to prevent the promoters from using their powers of deviation,[6] or to bind them in any other special way, should have appropriate clauses inserted in the special Act.[7]

(b.) *General Act.*

Mistakes in plans and books of reference.

Clause 7 of the Railway Clauses Consolidation Act[8] provides for the correction of mistakes in the plans and books of reference. With regard to this, Wood, V.-C., has said,[9] "I think the difficulty which was intended to be corrected by the 7th section of the Railways Clauses Act is, that

[5] *R.* v. *South Wales Railway Company*, 6 Rlwy. Ca. 489; *Oxford, Worcester, and Wolverhampton Railway Company* v. *South Staffordshire Railway Company*, 1 Dr. 255.

[6] Sects. 11 to 15 of General Act; see *Pearce* v. *Wycombe Railway Company*, 1 Dr. 244.

[7] *North British Railway Company* v. *Tod*, 12 Cl. & F. 722; *Leominster Canal Navigation* v. *Shrewsbury and Hereford Railway Company*, 3 K. & J. 654. Examples of such clauses may be found in *Eton College* v. *Great Western Railway Company*, 1 Rlwy. Ca. 200; *Gray* v. *Liverpool and Bury Railway Company*, 9 Beav. 391; *Sparrow* v. *Oxford, Worcester, and Wolverhampton Railway Company*, 9 Hare, 436; 2 D. M. G. 94; *St. Thomas's Hospital* v. *Charing Cross Railway Company*, 1 J. & H. 400.

[8] 8 & 9 Vict. c. 20.

[9] *Kemp* v. *West End Railway Company*, 1 K. & J. 689; *Taylor* v. *Clemson*, 2 Q. B. 978. Errors of this description are often very numerous. Report of Select Committee of the House of Lords on Compensating Landowners (1845), p. 23.

there might be some omission, either of the land in the plan, or of the owner in the book of reference, rendering identification difficult. Probably what was intended, *reddendo singula singulis*, was some omission of land in the plan, or of the owner, lessee, or occupier in the book of reference. The Act prescribes, that the land shall be marked on the plan, and the names of the owners be described in the book of reference. It might happen that the land might be marked on the plan, and all descriptions omitted in the book of reference, or there might possibly be no number, or a wrong acreage; and, at the same time, there might be coupled with such a statement a list of persons' names utterly incapable of affording any identification, from being entirely erroneous. This might happen from the repetition which sometimes occurs in transcribing, by the person copying putting into the next line the name of the person in the former line, or some error of that kind; and, therefore, the legislature seems to me to have meant no more than this, that where there should be such an erroneous description that the company cannot act on their general empowering clauses, because they cannot satisfy persons that the land in question was described in the plan and in the book of reference, they may then go before a magistrate to get that state of things corrected. I think the 7th section means no more than that; and I should be laying too much stress on the inferential view that that section may afford with reference to the construction of the 19th section of the special Act, if I were to say that the words are so plain as that this section can be modified in the manner which this 7th section indicates, as having been possibly the intention of the legislature that it should be modified. On the other hand, there are difficulties which are not inconsiderable, that may arise from this construction: a person might be omitted altogether as owner, and not have the slightest notice that his land is required, which seems to have been the case here; and the legislature may be misled by supposing that he is named in the book of reference, and that he has had notice. It turns out in point of fact that the plaintiffs here have not had any notice whatever, and knew nothing about it. However, I think if the legislature intended to obviate such an evil, that intention should have been more clearly pointed out than it is in these clauses, which do not, in my opinion, reach the evil, if such it be. In the case of actual fraud, I apprehend this Court would have jurisdiction to interfere. It has been held, that, notwithstanding an Act of Parliament, the Court may reach fraud in obtaining an Act of Parliament, or a judgment of the Court; but here no question of that kind arises: the case is simply one of negligence." The company were allowed to exercise their compulsory powers, although the names of the plaintiffs, who had a term in the property of 80 years, were altogether omitted from the book of reference, and there was reason to suppose that if they had had notice Parliament would have given them special protection.

Viaducts and tunnels. Clause 13.

By the 13th clause, where in any place it is intended to carry the railway on an arch or arches, or other viaduct, as marked on the plan, the same shall be made accordingly, no deviation being allowed; and similarly with respect to a tunnel.[1]

Bridges over roads.

Clause 49 provides, that bridges constructed

[1] *Little* v. *Newport and Hereford Railway Company*, 17 Jur. 209.

CHAP. IV.

Sect. 3.
Clause 49.

to carry the line over turnpike[2] and other roads, shall be of the span and height thereby provided according to the nature and width of the road.[3] The descent in the road, so as to carry the same under the bridge, is not to exceed certain gradients specified. It seems that no additional width is allowed for a footpath,[4] and that the company may lower a road without lowering the footpath, if that is the more beneficial course.[5]

Footpath.

Bridges over the line.

Clause 50 provides for the width of and ascent[6] to bridges, by which cross-roads are carried over the railway.[7]

[2] A turnpike road, is a road which is repaired by means of tolls collected upon it. *Northam Bridge and Roads* v. *London and Southampton Railway Company*, 6 M. & W. 428 ; 1 Rlwy. Ca. 653.

[3] *Attorney-General* v. *London and Southampton Railway Company*, 9 Sim. 78 ; 1 Rlwy. Ca. 302 ; *Wintle* v. *Bristol and South Wales Union Railway Company*, 10 W. R. 210. As to right of the company to construct temporary bridges during the progress of the works, see *London and Birmingham Railway Company* v. *Grand Junction Railway Company*, 1 Rlwy. Ca. 224 ; *Priestley* v. *Manchester and Leeds Railway Company*, 2 Rlwy. Ca. 134.

[4] *Re Rigby*, 19 L. J. Q. B. 153.

[5] *R.* v. *Manchester and Leeds Railway Company*, 3 Q. B. 528.

[6] *Attorney-General* v. *London and Southampton Railway Company*, 1 Rlwy. Ca. 283.

[7] *South Eastern Railway Company* v. *R.*, 20 L. J. Q. B. 428.

Approaches.

It appears that the company are not authorised under any circumstances to make the approaches to the bridges narrower than the corresponding parts of the road were before.[8]

It may be remarked that clause 14, prescribing certain gradients, levels, &c., refers to the construction of the line itself, and not to cross-roads.[9]

Roads.

Clause 53, *et seq.*

If the company find it necessary to interfere with any road, either public or private, so as to make it impassable for, or dangerous, or extraordinarily inconvenient to passengers or carriages, or to the persons entitled to the use thereof, they are first to provide a sufficient road in substitution[1] for it; and unless the original road is restored, the substituted road, or some other sufficient substituted road, is to be put into a permanently substantial condition, equally con-

[8] *R.* v. *London and Birmingham Railway Company*, 1 Rlwy. Ca. 317; *R.* v. *Birmingham and Gloucester Railway Company*, 2 Q. B. 47.

[9] *Beardmer* v. *London and North Western Railway Company*, 1 Mac. & Gor. 112; *R.* v. *Caledonian Railway Company*, 20 L. J. Q. B. 147.

[1] A road already existing was held not to be a substituted road under this section, *Attorney-General* v. *Great Northern Railway Company*, 4 De G. & S. 75.

Chap. IV. Sect. 3.

venient[2] as the former road, or as near thereto as circumstances will allow.[3]

Doing as little damage as can be.

It is provided by the 16th clause, that in the exercise of their powers, the company shall do as little damage as can be. As a general rule, the company, acting *bonâ fide*, are the judges of the most convenient mode of executing the works.[4] But Lord Lyndhurst restrained a company from making an arch of less than certain dimensions

[2] As a driftway as well as for passengers and carriages, *R.* v. *London and Birmingham Railway Company*, 1 Rlwy. Ca. 317.

[3] *Spencer* v. *London and Birmingham Railway Company*, 1 Rlwy. Ca. 159; *R.* v. *London and Birmingham Railway Company*, 1 Rlwy. Ca. 317; *Kemp* v. *London and Brighton Railway Company*, 1 Rlwy. Ca. 495; *London and Brighton Railway Company* v. *Blake*, 2 Rlwy. Ca. 322; *Attorney-General* v. *Eastern Counties Railway Company*, 3 Rlwy. Ca. 337; *Attorney-General* v. *London and South Western Railway Company*, 3 De G. & S. 439; *Bell* v. *Hull and Selby Railway Company*, 2 Rlwy. Ca. 279; *R.* v. *Scott*, 3 Q. B. 543; *Ellis* v. *South Western Railway Company*, 2 H. & N. 424; *Gawthorn* v. *Stockport, Disley, and Whaley Bridge Railway Company*, 3 Jur. N. S. 573; *Caledonian Railway Company* v. *Colt*, 3 Macq. 833; *Marquis of Salisbury* v. *Great Northern Railway Company*, 5 C. B. N. S. 174. This section does not refer to the conversion of a road into a railway, *Tanner* v. *South Wales Railway Company*, 1 Jur. N. S. 1215. As to who is to be considered an "owner" under these clauses, see *Collinson* v. *Newcastle and Darlington Railway Company*, 1 C. & K. 546; *Mann* v. *Great South and Western Railway*, 9 Ir. C. L. 105.

[4] *London and Birmingham Railway Company* v. *Grand Junction Canal Company*, 1 Rlwy. Ca. 225; *Priestley* v. *Manchester and Leeds Railway Company*, 2 Rlwy. Ca. 134; *R.* v. *Sharpe*, 3 Rlwy. Ca. 3[illegible]; see *Richards* v. *Richards*, J. 255.

over a mill-race.[5] And the Court will also interfere where there is a binding agreement respecting the construction of the works between a land-owner and the company.[6]

Company contracting itself out of its powers.

With reference, however, to such agreements, when not incorporated with the special Act, Lord Langdale said,[7] "I do not think it perfectly clear, that a company having a power given to it plainly for the public good, but which may effect an injury on an individual, in respect of which compensation can be given, has a right to contract itself out of those powers. On a proper occasion these matters ought to be most carefully considered. I certainly have never felt the least disposition to extend the powers of railway companies; and I believe it would be for their own and for the public advantage if these powers

[5] *Coats* v. *Clarence Railway Company*, 1 R. & M. 181; *Manser* v. *North Eastern Railway Company*, 2 Rlwy. Ca. 380; see *Attorney-General* v. *London and South Western Railway Company*, 3 De G. & S. 439; *Attorney-General* v. *Dorset Central Railway Company*, 3 L. T. N. S. 608.

[6] *Sanderson* v. *Cockermouth and Workington Railway Company*, 11 Beav. 497; on appeal, 19 L. J. Ch. 503; *Clarke* v. *Manchester, Sheffield, and Lincolnshire Railway Company*, 1 J. & H. 631.

[7] *Breynton* v. *London and North Western Railway Company*, 10 Beav. 238; 2 C. P. Coop. 108; see *Selby* v. *Colne Valley and Halsted Railway Company*, 10 W. R. 661.

Chap. IV.
Sect. 3.

were less than they seem to be; but if they have powers given them for the public benefit, such, for instance, as to make a road under instead of across a railway, I do not feel satisfied they have the right or power to contract themselves out of it by a private agreement with any individual whatever."

Application for Injunction.

Persons seeking to restrain the operations of a company in the construction of the works, are bound to be prompt in making their application. Where, after a company had opened the line for traffic, it was decided that a bridge should have been built where a certain road was crossed on a level, and the proprietors of the road moved for an injunction to stop the traffic, the motion was ordered to stand over upon the company undertaking to build a bridge forthwith.[9]

[8] *Shand* v. *Henderson*, 2 Dow. 519; *Greenhalgh* v. *Manchester and Birmingham Railway Company*, 9 Sim. 416; 3 My. & Cr. 784; *Graham* v. *Birkenhead, &c., Railway Company* 2 Mac. & Gor. 146; *Lind* v. *Isle of Wight Ferry Company*, 1 N. R. 13.

[9] *Proprietors of Northam Bridge and Roads* v. *London and Southampton Railway Company*, 1 Rlwy. Ca. 653.

INDEX.

THE END.

www.ingramcontent.com/pod-product-compliance
Lightning Source LLC
Chambersburg PA
CBHW031409270326
41929CB00010BA/1389
* 9 7 8 3 3 3 7 8 1 3 0 7 9 *